The Classic Guide to POLO

T. F. DALE

AMBERLEY

First edition published 1905

This edition first published 2015

Amberley Publishing
The Hill, Stroud
Gloucestershire, GL5 4EP

www.amberley-books.com

British Library Cataloguing in Publication Data.
A catalogue record for this book is available from the British Library.

ISBN 978 1 4456 4866 8 (print)
ISBN 978 1 4456 4867 5 (ebook)

Typesetting and Origination by Amberley Publishing.
Printed in the UK.

Contents

Contents

Editor's Note

Although nowadays most associated with Britain, India, Argentina and the USA, polo has a rather varied history. It is in fact an ancient sport and interestingly originated in Ancient Persia, spreading throughout the East before eventually arriving in the West via the Indian Subcontinent. From its beginnings polo was played by kings and courtiers. Polo helped improve the horses for cavalry and their riders' horsemanship. While the rules have changed, the premise of the game remains much the same as it did in Ancient Persia. When it was introduced to nineteenth-century Britain, it was referred to as 'hockey on horseback'. The two most influential clubs in the country were Ranelagh and Hurlingham, and the Hurlingham Polo Association today remains the governing body for the game in the UK, Ireland and many other countries.

Written in 1905 by Thomas Francis Dale, *Polo: Past and Present* covered the history of the sport from its early beginnings in the East to its eventual introduction to the West. Dale's observations and reflections also explore the principles and basics of polo, its rules, and the training and breeding of ponies. Hugely popular at the time of the guide's first publication, polo is still beloved today, with over seventy clubs in the UK alone. Although the modern world places less emphasis on class within sport as they did in Dale's time, his book is still as relevant to today's version of the game as it was in the early twentieth century.

Dale was a prolific writer and his works included *The Game of Polo* (1897) and *The History of the Belvoir Hunt* (1899). He was also steward and member of the Council of the Polo and Riding Pony Society. Having been trained at one of the best schools of polo in India, Dale was well versed in the sport and provides a thorough introduction to polo for readers past and present.

Vanessa Le
Editor
2015

1

Ancient Polo

Polo is perhaps the most ancient of games. When history was still legend we find polo flourishing. All our best games are derived from it, and cricket, golf, hockey, and the national Irish game of hurling are all descendants of polo. The historic order was reversed when in England polo on its first introduction was called 'hockey on horseback,' and in Ireland 'hurling on horseback'. In reality these games are polo on foot.

The cradle of polo was Persia, and from that country the game spread all over the East, taking root most firmly in India, and at Constantinople under the Byzantine Emperors.

It is very difficult to separate legend and history in the stories of Oriental lands - so much of the history is legendary, so many of the legends are historical. But, however we may puzzle over the succession and even the identity of the kings of the various dynasties, of one thing we may be absolutely sure, that from the earliest times to the eighteenth century there was always polo at the Persian court. Every Persian king either took part in the game or looked on while his courtiers played.

I have examined the various authorities in order to see if it was possible to reconstruct the old Persian polo from their writings. I felt that this would be more interesting than the mere record of the references to the game in the pages of poets and historians. So I have endeavoured to discover what their methods of play were, in the old days, what rules they played under, and in what ways the game varied or developed during successive periods and in different countries.

Persian polo differed from the game in other countries by the fact that it was a national sport. In the poetical histories or historical poems in which Persian literature is so rich, the heroes are often celebrated for their skill at polo. Nor are their victories in war or love described in language more high flown. This shows the esteem in which the game was held. The Persians were a nation of horsemen, and every Persian youth of rank was taught not merely to ride, but to be at home in the saddle. It has more than once occurred to me, while writing this chapter, as strange that polo, which must have been well known to the peoples that came in contact with the Persians – the Greeks, the Romans, and the English, – should never have made its way into their countries. The reason in all probability was the inferiority of the horsemanship of the Greeks and Romans, and the lack of suitable horses. The Persians on the other hand had in their horses light, active, well-bred animals of Arab type, and about 14.2 in height.

It seems likely that while the natural gift for, and acquired skill in horsemanship must have encouraged polo, this game improved the riding of the Persians and increased the efficiency of their cavalry. There is no such school of horsemanship as polo, especially for acquiring the strong, easy, confident seat that is desired for modern cavalry, according to the latest official instructions on their training. We speak, however, of polo generally, but there have been no less than five, or, including our modern game, six varieties of polo during its existence of at least 2000 years. Some of the variations in the game are considerable. For example, there was the Indian form known as *rôl*, which consisted in dribbling the ball along the ground, and the interest of which lay in keeping possession of it by means of dexterous turns and twists of a long stick; and the Byzantine form of the game, which I do not know better how to describe than by saying that it was a kind of la crosse on horseback. Of both these I shall have occasion to write later on.

In ancient polo there are only three constant things, the horse, the ball, and an instrument to strike the latter with. Everything else varied the number of players, the size of the ground, the height of the horses, the shape of the stick, and even the material of which the ball was made. This last has, at all events since the game made its way to the borders of Thibet, been known as polo from a Thibetan word signifying willow root, from which material our English polo balls are still turned. All polo balls were made of wood, except that in the twelfth century the ball used in Byzantine polo was either made of, or covered with leather.

The horse ridden was, I think, most commonly the ordinary Arab of about 14.2; but some ancient pictures show that two kinds of ponies were sometimes used – first the larger Arab, and secondly a small, active, somewhat coarse pony, which was probably a hill pony. It is of course quite possible that, like the modern pony breeder, the old Persian appreciated the value for polo of a cross of true pony blood. But, however that may be, the pictures are only evidence of the stamp of ponies used in the artist's own time.

The polo stick has varied very much, and as in our day there is no standard for the length of the stick, the shape of the head, or the angle at which the latter is fixed to the head, but each player uses the kind that suits him best, so in ancient times the shape and length of the stick varied greatly. The earliest form of which we know anything had a kind of spoon-shaped head, and this was probably not used, as one or two writers have suggested, for carrying the ball, but for those lofty strokes which, as we see from the account in the *Sháh-náma*, were much admired.

This shape of stick was a survival of a still earlier form of polo than has come down to us in the old pictures. I think it seems likely that the earliest game was simply a trial of skill with the stick and ball, that there were no limits to the ground nor were there any goals. The players simply tried to outdo each other in fancy strokes, such as hitting the ball into the air, striking or volleying it while flying. The struggle was for the possession of the ball, and those were adjudged the victors who showed most skill and address in the use of the stick and the management of their horses. The division into sides, the establishment of rules, and the erection of goals were later developments. The more orderly game soon modified the stick, which became first a hockey stick and then a hammer-headed mallet such as we have now. I imagine that the two forms of polo, the orderly game, and the exercise of skill in horsemanship and in the use of the stick, existed side by side for some time, and that we have accounts of both. In the earlier stage of the game a ball or balls were flung down and an unlimited number of young men exhibited their skill before the king and his court.

In the later phase sides were chosen, rules observed, and the game was played much as we play it now. There were also three ways of starting the game; the first and most ancient, which came from the primitive polo, is that retained in Manipur and Gilgit to this day. The chief man among the players gallops down carrying the ball till he reaches the middle of the ground, when he throws it up into the air and hits it flying.

A hit should be made from the centre of the ground, and a good man will often hit a goal. The starter on his side must be able to pick up the ball for the goal to count. The man who has hit the goal will throw himself off his pony and try to pick up the ball while the other side with fine impartiality hit him or the ball or ride over him in their endeavour to save the goal.

In this sentence I fancy I find another survival of ancient polo and that we have here one of the oldest rules of the game. If this was so it may be almost a source of wonder that polo never found its way into the Roman amphitheatre. A game by professionals with rules like this might have been exciting enough and sufficiently dangerous to make a Roman holiday. The ball was also from a very early time bowled in, much as our umpires do now, between the players drawn up in two ranks. The third way was to place the ball in the centre of the ground. The two sides were then drawn up, each on its respective back line, started at a signal and raced for the possession of the ball.

The grounds varied in size, but their surfaces were as carefully looked after as they are now. The Persian polo ground was sometimes twice as long as ours but seldom more than 170 yards in breadth. This shows us that polo must have been a fast-galloping game. On the other hand, the strokes used were much the same as ours, and players were particularly fond of the stroke under the pony's neck to the left front of the player. Long shots at the goal were then, as now, often attempted by the best players. The fixed goals show that they used an established ground. The posts were of stone, and, if we may judge by the old pictures, solidly and firmly built. This must have been dangerous, for we know that even the wooden posts used before the paper ones were introduced caused several accidents. On the other hand, we must remember that the Persians were extraordinarily skilful and practised horsemen of the Oriental type that their ponies were of Eastern breeds accustomed to stop and to wheel on their haunches, and were strongly bitted. No Oriental ever lets his horse out of his hand. His horse's hind legs are always well under him, and the Arab horse is from hereditary habit the handiest of animals, as those who have ridden him after a jinking hog know well. Thus the danger was less than it would be with English ponies. These permanent goal-posts were twenty-four feet apart, giving the same length of goal line as we have today. In the best ancient polo, as in our first-class matches in modern times, there were four players on each side. Combination and team-play were undoubtedly understood, as I shall presently show, and there were some very clearly defined rules.

It was certainly forbidden to stand over the ball, and perhaps to slacken speed before you hit it, but at all events it was considered bad form not to gallop. It was also thought to be bad play to hang about outside the game for the chance of a run, and I think that about the tenth century there was a rule which forbade offside. When I write of rules I do not of course know if there was a written code, but it is certain there was a traditional form of rules and etiquette handed down and strictly adhered to.

Polo was taken very seriously in Persia and India. Skill and address at the game were recommendations to promotion at court. It was thought that polo was a game that showed the character of the player and tested his temper, courage, and disposition. The Emperor Akbar watched his young nobles and soldiers at the game, and formed his conclusions as to their fitness for service from their demeanour. Certainly we have reason to think after the experience of our last war in South Africa that such a method of selection would not work badly.

Now let us turn to the authorities on which these conclusions as to ancient polo are based. It is one of the facts which show us how deeply polo was rooted as a national sport in the affections of the Persians, that allusions to it are so frequent in their poets. The Persians loved and indeed still love poetry greatly, and therefore polo must have been thoroughly known and understood, since it is so often used in the metaphors of the poets, and references to the game are continual. Indeed, one mystic poem is called 'Stick and Ball.' It would occupy too much space to compile an anthology of polo from the Persian poets. But we may note some of the more remarkable passages on which I have based my reconstruction of ancient polo. And perhaps I cannot begin better than by a translation and commentary on the account of the first recorded international polo match. This is taken from the *Sháh-náma*, the *Iliad* of Persia. This match was played perhaps at Tashkend between the Iranians and the Turanians. It is interesting to note that the inhabitants of the two countries, though constantly at war, are supposed by the poet to be equally well acquainted with the game, and to have had a common code of rules. The occasion of the match was as follows: – Siawusch, a Persian prince, had taken refuge at the court of Afrāsiāb, king of the Turks, having fallen into disgrace at his father's court, a woman being, as usual in the East, at the bottom of the mischief. Even though Siawusch had proved his innocence by passing through the ordeal of fire, yet the lady's word was taken against his, and the young prince went into exile.

With some faithful companions he took refuge at the court of Afrāsiāb, the hereditary foe of his race and family, and was by him well received and treated. Were they not both keen polo players? No doubt Afrāsiāb saw in the arrival of the Persians the prospect of an unusually interesting match. The king gave them a week to rest the ponies in, and then one night after dinner he proposed to Siawusch a polo match in the morning. 'I have always heard,' he added,' what a great player you are, and that when you hit the ball no one else has a chance.' To which Siawusch replies that he is quite sure that in polo as in everything else the king is his superior, and then follows half a page of an exchange of elaborate compliments. Neither, however, as will be seen, meant to throw away a chance of winning. In the morning the players were early on the ground in the highest spirits, galloping their ponies and knocking the ball about. Then the king proposed to Siawusch a 'pick up' game, each to choose six men from Afrāsiāb's followers. Siawusch was too good a courtier to permit this, and he begs the king to allow him to play on the same side as his majesty. 'If indeed you think me good enough,' says the prince with a modest politeness. But the king, resolved not to be done out of his game, hints that he is determined to have a match, reminds the prince that his reputation as a player is at stake, and urges that on his side he wants to test his visitor's skill. On this Siawusch yields and the king arranges the sides, picking out the best players for himself, especially Nestiken, 'wonderfully keen at riding off,' and Human, 'noted for his control of the ball.' To Siawusch he only gave the hard riders, and the prince was not disposed to acquiesce.

He objects that this will never do, and that the king's own men will not support a stranger: 'I shall be left to hit the ball alone.' Then comes a passage from which I infer two things – first, that polo had in those early days a code of rules common to the different countries in Asia in which it was played; secondly, that' team ' play or combination was appreciated and practised. For Siawusch was anxious to have his own team, and begged to be allowed to bring on to the ground his Persian followers, 'who will play in combination with me according to the rules of international polo.' I am not quite sure that the king was pleased – 'he listened and agreed,' is the curt remark of the poet, and this is in contrast to the flow of compliments that had taken place when King Afrāsiāb thought he was going to have things his own way. Siawusch then picks six first-class players. They played apparently seven aside.

'Then the band began to play, and the air was filled with dust,' which will recall familiar experiences to Anglo-Indian players.' You would have thought there was an earthquake, so great was the noise of trumpets and cymbals.' This is quite the Oriental idea of a band.

The king started the game by bowling in the ball, which we are told he did 'in the correct manner,' here again giving a trace of a rule. Siawusch was quick on it and before it had touched the ground skied the ball in true Oriental style, hitting so hard that it was lost. Then the mighty king ordered another ball to be brought to Siawusch (new ball, umpire!). The prince took it, kissed it (the band began to play cymbals and drums *da capo*), Siawusch changed ponies, and this time himself started the game by throwing the ball into the air and hitting it flying. He was a hard hitter and something of a gallery player, but he thoroughly enjoyed the game. 'His face glowed with pleasure and excitement,' says the poet. Every one said they had never seen such a horseman and player as the prince, and the king observed that his play and his good looks, which latter gift by the way was the cause of his exile – exceeded even the report he had heard of him.

Then, after this exhibition play, the real international match began, Afrāsiāb and Siawusch looking on while their respective followers played in the great match Iran *v.* Turan. There was a fast, well - fought game. 'Now one side, now another held possession of the ball, and the air was full of dust and Persian expletives.' The Turks had the worst of it and lost their tempers. Siawusch was rather alarmed and was angry with his followers for their injudicious conduct. He spoke in Pahlavi, a curious ancient language of the sixth century, written in an Aramaic character and with a Persian pronunciation. This was not understanded of the Turks. 'Do you forget that you are only playing a game, not fighting a battle?' he said. 'As soon as the game is finished' – even discretion would not bring them away, we see, until the call of 'Time!'–'come away and leave the ball to the Turks.' The Persian players took a pull and from that moment, we are told, they gave their ponies an easy time. 'The Turks after this had the game much to themselves.' But Afrāsiāb was too good a player not to understand that his side was beaten. I am glad to be able to say that the Turks forgot their ill feeling and drank Siawusch's health at dinner like sportsmen.

Other traces of the game are found in the historical romance of *Ardishir* (written in Pahlavi) where there are references to polo, and we are told that the conqueror's military exploits were foreshadowed by his successes in the polo field. Then Bahram IV, whose exploits are also narrated in the *Sháh-náma*, had tutors to teach him reading, hunting, and polo. I gather from his history that the last two were more successful than the first. He was a jovial, hearty sportsman of a type more popular with the people than approved by historians. One of the most interesting references to polo is to be found in Nizámí, a poet who flourished about the middle of the twelfth century – and in this case we are on firm historic ground. Khusru Parvez (or the conqueror) appears in Gibbon (*Decline and Fall*, ch. XLVI) as Chosroes II. He was restored to his throne by the Emperor Maurice of Byzantium at the end of the sixth century of our era. He was a Zoroastrian, but his queen, Shírín, was a Roman by birth and a Christian by religion. The Greek historians say that she was a daughter of the Emperor Maurice, who was of Roman descent. She was a woman of beauty and brains, and she had great ascendency over Khusru, whose passion for her is the subject of a poem only second in interest to the *Sháh-náma*.

Khusru and Shírín's peace was somewhat troubled by the queen's fancy for a youth, by name Ferhad, and by Gurdiya who afterwards married Khusru, in spite of Shírín's efforts to prevent it. The point which interests us is that not only Khusra and Ferhad but also Shinn, Gurdiya, and their attendant ladies were polo players. The ladies rode, however, cavalier fashion, and sat in their saddles like Cypresses – the true easy polo seat. This is said of the seventy veiled maidens who accompanied Shírín to the presence of the king. Having heard that their skill in archery and polo was equal to their looks, the king started for the polo ground, more, however, to see the ladies than their polo – With happy heart in order to behold these '*houris.*' When, however, the king saw that they really could hit the ball he joined in the game. Perhaps also as the ladies wore black veils he wished to have a closer view. As there were seventy of them I suggest that this was an exercise of skill with the ball rather than a regular game. It represented in fact the older form of polo that survived side by side with the more scientific game that had developed out of it. But I have another suggestion to make: polo is a rough game for women, and especially for those who, like the ladies of the East, have their face for their fortune. What I think is that Shírín and her ladies were playing the Byzantine form of the game, which depended upon skill and horsemanship rather than force and strength.

I have before me an account of a polo match played at Byzantium in the reign of Manuel Comnenus, and told by his faithful secretary Cinnamus. Manuel came to the throne of Constantinople AD. 1143. His exploits in war and in the arena, the jousts in which he overcame the flower of the Italian chivalry, and his many conquests, made him a popular hero in Asia as well as Europe, and thus Nizámí was doubtless familiar with his fame. The Emperor Manuel had a fall at polo which incapacitated him for active service for a time, and to this we owe our knowledge of Byzantine polo. Cinnamus tells his story thus:

In the winter the emperor devoted himself to an ancient and honourable sport, which is of great antiquity and reckoned suitable from days of old for royal personages. The manner of the game is as follows: The young men divide into two parties equal in number and betake themselves to a ground which had aforetime been laid out carefully. They use a leathern ball about the size of an apple. This ball being placed in the middle of the ground (possibly they rode for it, as was the old Anglo-Indian custom, each side starting from its own goal line) – the players contend for it for a prize. In their right hands they hold a stick of moderate length with a round racquet at the end. Across the racquet strings are stretched in a close network. The object of the game is to drive the ball over a goal line measured beforehand. That party which with the racquet drives the ball oftenest over the goal line wins. This game is rather dangerous, and falls are frequent. It is necessary for a player to bend this way and that, and to turn his pony in a circle or indeed in any direction that the flight of the ball may render necessary.' Then the historian goes on to tell how the emperor trying to turn his pony too sharply – how often have we not seen players throw their ponies in this way – the animal came down and rolled over him. Although the emperor remounted and tried to go on, he was found to be suffering from an injured thigh and a slight concussion.

Now here we have an account of polo from a trustworthy historian. I suggest, however, that it was this form of polo, less rough than the Persian form, that Nizámí imagined Shírín and her ladies to have played, and that Shírín brought this form of the game with her from Constantinople. From the story of Shírín I gather that polo for women was a novelty at the court of Chosroes II. Later Gurdiya and Shírín seem to have played a polo match for the king's affections, and the former to have been so far successful that the king married her even in spite of Shírín's warning that Gurdiya, of whose prowess in the game she was possibly jealous, was a 'she devil.'

But a point of interest arises now that polo is coming into the clear light of history. How old is the game? It is evident that the poets believed polo to be most ancient. But Firdousi and Nizámí could only have written of the game as they knew it, and thus the accounts above really belong to a period not earlier than the tenth century of our era. Yet

Polo in Japanese and
Byzantine, form of
stick, leathern ball.

no doubt the game was much older. I regard the accounts
in the *Sháh-náma* as representing the oldest orderly form
of polo. Firdousi came of one of those old Persian gentle
families who were particularly careful in the preservation of
their traditions. Like our own Walter Scott, Firdousi's mind,
long before he wrote his great poem, was stored with the
legends, ballads, songs, and poems of old Persia. Tradition
in the East is permanent and persistent, and in Persia above
all, so that it is probably no exaggeration when we assert
the game to have an antiquity of two thousand years. Of
course, at what period it developed from being an exercise
of horsemanship to a scientific game with sides and rules,
no one can say. All that we know is that we find polo in
the tenth century a highly organised game, with a code of
rules common to several countries.

When once we reach historic times the rules and histories of the game of polo are more easily ascertained. In another old Persian poem there are traces of an offside rule, the players were four a-side, and there was a' back' with well-defined duties, and I think from this we may infer that the other places in the game were not dissimilar to ours, and that there was combination as well as individual play. Selfish play was, it is evident, well known and condemned, as the ironic advice in the following passage may show:

> When the ball comes to you hit it back into the game and pretend to ride hard after it, but do not go into the scrimmage. Keep at a safe distance and take care of yourself.

In the fifteenth and sixteenth centuries the game had spread from Persia to Central Asia and Thibet, and was popular in Central India. The Emperor Akbar valued the game because it both made horsemen of the riders and taught their chargers to be handy. Thus it is also probable that from 14 to 15 hands was polo height in India in the sixteenth century. They played five-a-side, as we used to do in India and England when the game was first introduced among Englishmen. The two forms of the game, the dribbling and the hard-hitting, were both recognised. The mallet was hammer-headed, and the ground was in Persia certainly, as in India probably, about the same size as ours. Sir Anthony Shirley says the polo ground of Ispahan occupied a space of ten acres, and was most carefully levelled. In some of the old pictures of Eastern polo the kings and warriors are represented playing on a too flowery mead, which caused a friend of mine to observe that with the grass so long the game must have been very sticky. I think, however, the flowers may be considered to be an artistic licence and intended by the courtly painters as a compliment to the kings and great men, under whose horses' feet flowers might naturally be expected to spring up.

By this time the strokes familiar to us now – forward and back-handed, as well as the cut under the pony's tail, and the near-side stroke under its belly by which I have seen Hîra Singh make many a goal – were all well known. Political troubles drove the game out of Persia and India. It lingered only on the borders of Thibet in the rough-and-ready form described by Colonel Algernon Durand, and in Manipur. From Manipur it was introduced among the indigo planters. Then polo travelled to Calcutta, and at last, one summer afternoon at Shorncliffe, the first game was played in England by the 10th Hussars. Since then its growth has been rapid, and it has travelled back from England to Persia. Major P. M. Sykes thus tells of the reintroduction of polo into its native land.

In 1897 I brought sticks and balls to the capital, but was assured that no one would play. However, aided by Mr Horace Rumbold, who, by a coincidence, had played at Cairo with 'The Bays' (Major Sykes's own regiment), a trial game was organised, and shortly after the Legation was full of both players and ponies. I have since organised the game at Shiraz and Kirman, while players who learned at Teheran have established clubs at Vienna and Constantinople.

Polo has also a great antiquity in Japan. Mr K. Takahashi, of the Japanese Legation, informs me that he considers the game is at least a thousand years old in that country. It was very popular in the feudal period, not only among the Samurais, but also among the people. It is still, under the name of Da-kiu, or 'ball match,' a favourite game in Japan.

To sum up this chapter we may note that we have no historic references to early polo in any author previous to the tenth century. While such poetic writers as Firdousi (AD 941–1020) represent to us traditions of ages long before their time, and are evidence of the existence of a stick- and-ball game played on horseback in prehistoric times, yet the details of the games as described in the poems are probably those of their own day. The poet in describing the match in which Siawusch played, probably presented for us a polo match as he had seen it, and while we may readily believe in a much earlier popularity of polo in some form or other, yet we can only recover the rules of the game and the methods of play from the tenth century onwards.

My own view is that the earliest polo was an exercise of horsemanship, and continued in this form as a popular sport for a long period. The highly organised game described by Firdousi and other writers was chiefly played at the courts of kings. At all events we can, starting from Firdousi, trace the development of polo onwards.

The game was started – (1) by bowling in the ball; (2) by the captain of one side galloping from the back line carrying the ball to the centre, throwing it up, and hitting it flying; (3) by placing the ball on the ground in the centre, each side then galloping for it from their back line. (This was the way we started a game in India in 1879.) The sides were usually seven, five, or four in number, divided into a goalkeeper and forwards. If there was no offside the goalkeeper must have kept well back, as he did in India twenty years ago, and does still in America.

But I think that offside, if not made the subject of a rule, was in some cases restrained by the public opinion of polo-players. Combination and team-play was recognised, and a chief trained his followers and captained a team exactly as the princes of Patiala, Dholepur, and Jodhpur do today. Two kinds of horses were used, a smaller pony and the ordinary Arab charger. The strokes were the same as those in use today.

In the twelfth century the Byzantine form of the game, played with a racquet and leathern ball, seems to have been fashionable, and to have been played by women as well as men. It was the favourite sport of the Comneni, one of the ablest of the Byzantine dynasties.

In the sixteenth century the Emperor Akbar not only played the game, but regarded it as a serious exercise and a test of temper and courage for his younger courtiers. By this time there were two recognised styles of play – possibly they were two forms of the game – dribbling and hard-hitting; and sometimes one, sometimes the other was adopted by consent of the players beforehand.

In the seventeenth century, when Sir Anthony Shirley saw the game at the court of Shah Abbas, the grounds were about 300 by 170 yards and carefully levelled and kept in order, and the style of play was like that of the rough football of the Stuart period in England.

Chardin later in the seventeenth century saw what was evidently from his account a highly organised game, with rules against standing over the ball, or checking the pony. Speed had perhaps by this time become of more account than skill.

There have been six kinds of sticks used: (a) the stick with a spoon-shaped head, curved like a hockey stick; (b) the hockey-stick shape; (c) the long hammer-headed stick used in the dribbling game; (d) the shorter hammer-headed stick of which ours is the direct descendant; (e) the racquet; (f) the stick we use to-day, about 50 to 53 inches in length, with a cigar-shaped or square head.

There have been three kinds of ball: (a) the willow root; (b) the bamboo root; and (c) the leathern ball.

Goal-posts have been of stone, of wood, and are to-day of paper, but have always been 24 feet apart.

The grounds have generally been about the same size. The breadth has varied little, being about 200 yards or narrower, but the length has been sometimes, though rarely, double what it is now.

As to rules, we have seen that there was a common or international code, so that Persians and Turks played with much the same rules, written or unwritten, and could understand each other's play though they did not understand each other's language. But just as at Hurlingham, in the early days of polo, the game was governed more by the good feeling of players and a certain etiquette than by any code of rules, so I imagine it to have been among the Persians. Etiquette in the East would, it must be remembered, be a more controlling power than with ourselves.

It is probable that polo, after political troubles had driven it out of Persia and India and confined it to barbarous hill tribes, lost many of its rules and its civilised aspect. Thus in restoring it to the rank of a well-ordered and scientific game, we have merely brought polo back to what it was in its golden days in Persia.

2

The Hurlingham Club and Its Influence on Polo

The Hurlingham Club is known by name wherever polo is played. The rules drawn up by the Polo Committee are observed everywhere, except in India and America. Even the rules which govern the game in those countries are rather variations of the Hurlingham rules than distinct codes, and the changes made at Fulham are carefully considered at Lucknow and New York by the Indian and American polo associations.

The Hurlingham Club was founded by Mr Frank Heath cote in 1869, as a meeting-place for those pigeon-shooters who had been obliged to give up their old resorts owing to the invasion of bricks and mortar. Two years before the establishment of Hurlingham the Old Red House at Battersea, and Hornsey-Wood House, which had been in turn the headquarters of pigeon-shooting, were given over to the builders. Mr Frank Heath cote, who was at that time the organiser of most of the shooting competitions, chanced to hear that Mr R. C. Naylor was willing to let Hurlingham Park. A lease was granted in 1868, and the club was founded which has become the pattern and, as it were, the parent of many similar associations. As a pigeon-shooting resort the Hurlingham Club began, and so remained until the management was entrusted to Captain the Hon. J. D. Monson, afterwards eighth Lord Monson.

The Champion Cup at Hurlingham. A run on the ball.

Inter-regimental polo tournament at Hurlingham.

Captain Monson resolved to develop the social side of the Club. A new attraction was wanted, and polo was thought of. Captain Monson seems to have seen the possibilities of the game, and to his foresight much of its present success is due. In the earlier years of Captain Monson's managership the freehold of Hurlingham Park was bought, and within a very few years the property had doubled in value. In 1879 the Club purchased Mulgrave House with twenty acres of land. On this property, formerly in the occupation of the last Lord Ranelagh is the lake that is so picturesque a feature in the grounds. With Captain Monson was associated Captain, now Sir Walter, Smythe of Acton Burnell, and Mr Hurrell, who is still the secretary of the Club.

Hurlingham is picturesquely situated on the banks of the Thames at Fulham. The house, though of no very great antiquity, has an air of old-world comfort and solidity, not unbefitting the bankers and merchants who inhabited it in its earlier days. The gardens are delightful, and there is no pleasanter place nor a gayer or more picturesque scene than the lawn in front of Hurlingham House on a fine Saturday afternoon in May or June. One of the glories of Hurlingham is in its trees, and particularly the magnificent clumps of chestnuts that have given the name of the 'chestnuts goal' to a spot on the polo ground where many a keen struggle has taken place. But those who look over the green expanse of the polo ground can have little idea of the labour and difficulty that thirty years ago (1873) were undergone to make it. The famous match ground occupies the site of the orchard of the old house. Trees had to be cut down and uprooted. Nothing but great care and skill could have enabled Mr Sutherland, the head gardener, under the guidance of Captain Walter Smythe, to make the turf ground which has since been the scene of so many famous matches. Up to 1879 it was the only polo ground in London, and it long remained without a rival. It was at Hurlingham that 'guards' were first introduced along the sides of the ground, doubtless at first simply with the view of remedying the defects in the game caused by the limited size and irregular shape of the ground.

The Hurlingham polo field has been much enlarged since its early days, but the boards still remain. Indeed, to have a boarded ground is now all but a necessity to any first-class club England. These boards, which run down the sides of the parallelogram that a polo ground should be, have altered and probably greatly improved the game. But at all events it will be granted that the boards, which were unwillingly adopted at first, have influenced the development of polo in England and America in no slight degree. The success of the game when Hurlingham provided it with a place and a set of rules was immediate. The Club prospered greatly on its social side. The Prince of Wales (now HM Edward VII) gave it his countenance and support, and, in spite of an exclusive ballot, by 1882 the Hurlingham Club had a membership of fifteen hundred. Elections were held every Saturday, and a long list of candidates was waiting for admission.

The vouchers by which the friends of members were admitted were eagerly sought for, and to drive down to polo at Hurlingham became a regular part of the programme of those who would take part in a London season. Of course, only a fraction of the members were polo players, for Hurlingham is and has always been, almost from its beginning, one of the most-sought-after of social clubs. But Captain Monson and Captain Smythe had made no mistake when they foresaw and provided for the attractiveness of polo as a spectacle. They designed the pavilion, which was the finest of its kind when it was put up. This building, though it has often been enlarged, is acknowledged to be far too small for the present needs of the Club. It is said that some members of the Club and even of the Committee looked upon this stand as an extravagance. The fact is polo was regarded in those early days as a passing fashion, and too costly ever to become popular. It is called by a journalist in the 'seventies' a 'patrician sport.' We know now that it is nothing of the kind, but a game which has found considerable and widespread popularity among those of many classes who are interested in sports. For a long time, even within the polo memory of the author, the committees of clubs not wholly given to polo had hardly grasped its importance and attractiveness. Nor are they to be blamed for this. No one, not even the most enthusiastic admirer of the game, could have foreseen its present position. To the old Hurlingham Committee the polo members of the Club were a minority, always demanding a larger share of labour and expenditure than they were entitled to. At Hurlingham the pigeon-shooters who had been in possession there for some years regarded the polo players as a secondary and intrusive element in the club. The polo players regarded pigeon-shooting as an antiquated and not too defensible form of recreation, and cast envious eyes on the enclosure which would have been a most acceptable addition to the area of the polo ground.

There can, however, be no doubt that the game of polo owes its existence in England to the Hurlingham polo ground. This is an irregular oval with a surface of smooth turf, with a slight undulation towards the centre. The contour of the surface and its irregular shape, which Major Egerton Green and Mr St Quintin have greatly modified and improved, made the Hurlingham ground somewhat tricky in appearance, but I am bound to say, after watching many matches with a critical eye, I could never discover that the apparent defects in any way spoilt the interest of the game. Indeed, when we have eight rigidly drilled players riding eight perfectly schooled ponies and playing on an accurate parallelogram laid with the smoothest turf, as level as a golf green and as true as a billiard table, we may find that the game has lost some of its interest, and turn back again for the old thrill and excitement to Hurlingham and its irregularly shaped ground. But at all events when Captain Smythe opened the ground for play he at once secured the popularity of the game.

But we owe more than this to the Committee of Hurlingham. Not only did they start the game, but they gave it a code of rules. Although, as is noted elsewhere, the game was not played first at Hurlingham, yet before 1874 it only consisted in knocking about a ball. It looked like and was sometimes called hockey on horseback. Everything about the game was uncertain: the size of the ponies, the composition of the ball, the shape of the mallets. But the Hurlingham Committee took this in hand and produced a simple and effective code of rules, and by that means gave to the game of polo regularity and a prospect of permanence. No game can last if the aspiration of the chairman of a City dinner for a more liberal State Church is realised, and every man 'does that which is right in his own eyes.'

These rules I present here so that my readers can judge for themselves how this game has developed.

THE HURLINGHAM CLUB RULES OF POLO

1. The height of the ponies must not exceed 14 hands, and no ponies showing vice are to be allowed in the game.
2. The goals to be not less than 250 yards apart, and each goal to be 8 yards wide.
3. No spurs to be allowed with rowels, except on special occasions, when sanctioned by the Committee.
4. Each side shall nominate an umpire, unless it be mutually agreed to play with one instead of two; but his or their decisions shall be final.
5. None but proper sticks and balls approved by the Committee allowed. The size of the balls is decided to be three inches in diameter.
6. Should a player break his stick, or have it broken, he must ride to the appointed place where the sticks are kept, and take one.
7. In the event of a stick being dropped, the player must

dismount to pick it up; but he cannot strike the ball when dismounted.

8. A player may interpose his pony before his antagonist, so as to prevent the latter reaching the ball, whether in full career or otherwise; but may not cross another player in possession of the ball, unless at such a distance as to avoid all possibility of a collision.

9. It is allowed to hook an adversary's stick, but neither under or over an adversary's pony.

10. If a player is 'before his side' – i.e. he is in front of the player of his own side who hit the ball, but has not two of the opposite side between him and the hostile goal, and has not come through the bully – he is 'offside' or sneaking, and out of the game, and does not become' on his side' till the ball be hit or hit at by the opposite side, or until the player on his own side, who makes the hit, passes him. The player, until he is on his side, has no business to impede in any manner one of the opposing side.

11. If the ball is hit above the top of the goal posts, but in the opinion of the umpire through, it shall be considered a goal.

12. When the ball is hit beyond the goal and not through, the side defending the goal is entitled to a hit-off, which must be from the line.

13. When the ball is hit out of bounds, it must be thrown into the playground by an impartial person.

14. Each side to take up its position behind the goal posts, and on the flag being dropped the game commences.

15. The dress of the Hurlingham Club shall be light blue jerseys or shirts, blue forage caps, with silver band, light blue belts, butcher boots, and breeches. The second colours are white shirt or jersey. A pattern of the same can be seen on application to the secretary.

16. Each pony is to be passed under the standard by the Secretary or one of the Committee. A registered book to

be kept by the Secretary, in which the height of all ponies belonging to members is to be entered.

17. No person allowed within the arena (players and umpires excepted) under any circumstances whatever.

BYE-LAWS

1. From and after this date, the duration of games in all matches shall be for one hour and ten minutes; and there shall be an interval of five minutes between each twenty minutes of play.

2. The Polo ground shall be open for play, for not less than six players, at three o'clock each day, Fridays excepted, when the ground is closed. All play shall cease and the ground be cleared by 7.15.

3. Every pony that plays on the ground must be passed under the standard by the Secretary or one of the Polo Committee, and the same be entered in a book kept for the purpose. A pony passed under the standard as to regulation height, after he is aged, is permanently passed.

4. Not more than five players are allowed to play on each side in any game, the members who arrive first at the pavilion being allowed precedence.

5. Each set of players will be allowed the use of the ground for twenty-five minutes.

6. Colours must be worn in all games to distinguish sides. A set of broad red sashes will be kept in the office by the Secretary.

7. The competition for the Open Cup will be for five-a-side; for the Military Cup, four a-side.

Rule 33: The Shooting Season shall commence on the 5th of April, and end on the Monday in Goodwood race week, in each year. The Polo Season shall commence on the 1st of May, and end on a day fixed by the Committee, after a fortnight's notice thereof. The Committee shall have the power of opening the Club for any winter amusement that may hereafter be considered advisable, and to close the Polo ground on any day or days when, in their opinion, the state of the ground will not admit of the game being played without permanent injury to the turf. Under such circumstances, all possible notice shall be given by the Secretary.

The above rules were those under which the game grew and prospered. To them we owe the fact that scientific polo exists, and that having been once started it was placed on a firm and satisfactory basis.

The polo ground was ready, the game was being organised, but all would have been of no avail unless there had been players to support it. I can well remember the game as I saw it in England, and played it in India in its earlier days. The English game was in advance of the Indian one in science and tactics at first, and at Hurlingham they had given up the dribbling game some years before we did so in India, or, at any rate, in that part of India, the Bombay Presidency, with which I was then acquainted. Small ponies, a heavy short stick, no places kept except that of goalkeeper – it must be remembered that in early days there were five players on each side led to a slow dribbling game. Backhanders were quite a matter of choice, and hustling, apart from riding off as we understand it, was freely permitted. Umpires were not known except in first-class matches. There was a good deal of tumbling about, and scrimmages were frequent. The game was started by placing the ball in the centre of the ground. Then the opposing sides rode in for it from their respective goal lines, which was an exciting but dangerous feature. Later the players crossed sticks over the ball and then there was a good deal of clawing and snatching before the game fairly opened, in very many cases with scrimmages.

It may seem strange to players accustomed to our modern

Hurlingham Club house. Garden front.

Hurlingham polo pavilion.

methods of play, but we most of us formed our attachment to the game as it was played then. Polo was inferior to the scientific game of today, but it was very good fun all the same. However, we could not have played the game of today, for the ponies were not forthcoming. The early idea was that any scrambling pony would do for a conveyance. The ponies themselves corrected that idea, for the possession of well-trained, well-broken ponies was soon found to be an immense advantage. Then some players began to rise to prominence. The Messrs. Murrietta, who were well known at Market Harborough as hard riders across High Leicestershire, were perhaps the foremost players at Hurlingham of that period. Then there were the late Lord Queensberry, Mr R. Herbert of Clytha, Lords Cole and Casdereagh, all afterwards to be masters of hounds. But three of the men who were destined later to develop polo were gaining knowledge of the theory of the game, and skill in its practice at the International Gun and Polo Club at Brighton. There were first-rate matches played at Preston Park in the autumn of 1874. The two players who did most for the game at this time were Mr A. E. Peat and Mr E. Kenyon Stow. Both grasped the necessity of having trained ponies that could gallop. They sat down in their saddles instead of leaning forward, and they played with a straight arm, using the speed of the pony to give impetus to the ball. Thus when these players took the ball men who clung to the old dribbling style never saw it again, unless they caught a glimpse of it flying through the posts.

But like all innovations the new style of play did not become general all at once. It was not quite yet that the Peats and Mr Kenyon Stow were to make their appearance at Hurlingham, where, in the meantime, were practising Mr F. Mildmay, Mr Cumberland Bentley, Mr H. B. Patton, and Mr A. Greville. The 5th and 16th Lancers and the 1st Life Guards had also formed regimental teams, which made their appearance at Hurlingham and by their play raised the reputation of the Club and increased the popularity of polo. If we look over the old code of rules we shall see that although simple compared with the existing ones, yet that they contained everything necessary to regulate the game at that time. The alterations that have been made since are rather in the nature of explanations and definitions than of organic change. The rapid increase in the pace at which polo was played made it desirable that there should be some precautionary rules in order to render the game less dangerous. Many of the modern provisions for fouls and penalties are simply the old unwritten code that prevailed when the game was only played at a few clubs, and for the most part by men who knew one another more or less intimately. It was needless to warn men of errors which were understood to be against the spirit of the game. Cases of unfair riding off, of offside, of fouls, of unnecessary stick crooking were rare, if not unknown.

I can scarcely remember hearing the umpire's whistle in the earlier days, and I recollect having it pointed out to me on one occasion when I was learning the game in 1879 that an adversary's stick should not be crooked unless he was in the act of hitting the ball.

This indeed was in India, but the same thing has been told me by early players in England, and if from this first code we miss the penalties that are now laid down, it was because the offences were restrained by an unwritten code of honour among the players. Now this is not meant to imply that unfair play is at all common at polo now, but simply that the number of those playing has grown so large that the unwritten code of a club to which many of the players do not and could not belong, is obviously insufficient for regulation and restraint.

The first set of rules of 1873 was intended for the members of the Hurlingham Club. Other clubs were at liberty to adopt them or to modify them as they pleased. There was no idea in the minds of the first Hurlingham Polo Committee of exercising any authority outside the limits of their own enclosure. The last edition published this year (1905) was intended to apply to every polo club in England, and at least to be a standard for the colonies. True, the earlier clubs looked up to Hurlingham; it was the oldest and the largest. Indeed, most of the other clubs included a majority of Hurlingham members. The club at Brighton, the Monmouthshire, the Edinburgh, were founded to give increased opportunities of play to men who for two or three months played in London. In the same way Ireland accepted Hurlingham rules. Their greatest player, and indeed the re-constructor of the game, Mr John Watson, was a leading member of the Hurlingham Committee. The progress of the game was very rapid, and was due to its own intrinsic attractiveness, as well as to the arrangement of tournaments by Captain Smythe. The open Champion Cup was an obvious idea, but the Inter-Regimental Cup was a happy thought which, if it was suggested by the popularity of polo among soldiers, has also reacted on the game in the Army. The County Cup tournament, the matches between Oxford and Cambridge, Eton and Harrow, Lords and Commons, and later the Social Clubs Cup and the Handicap tournaments, have all done much to increase public interest in polo, and to improve play throughout the country.

For nearly twenty years the Hurlingham Club remained without a rival, and during that time it is not too much to say that scarcely a match of importance was played in England except on the ground at Hurlingham. There was but one ground, and two or three matches a week for some months in the year sufficed. If you wanted to see the very best play you looked on at the members' games. The players were the men who taught us by precept and example what a fine game polo was when played by the Messrs. Peat, Mr Kenyon Stow, Mr F. Mildmay, Mr T. Kennedy, who began late but quickly gained a high place among players, Lord Harrington, Mr John Watson, Captain F. Herbert, Captain Cecil Peters, and others. It seems to me as I look back that there never was quite so brilliant a forward as Mr J. E. Peat, so loyal a man to play for his side as Lord Harrington, such keen riders or true hitters as Mr Kenyon Stow and Mr Mildmay. I am

sure that there never was a back who combined tactics and
control alike of the ball and of his team to the same degree
as Mr John Watson. The art of making the most of the team
of which he was captain has never since been achieved in an
equal degree. In exhortation, rebuke, or encouragement he
was, and is unrivalled, although in later years the last named
bears a much greater proportion to the whole than it used
to do. He taught us the value of the backhander and how to
use it, and no one ever scorned gallery play more completely.

These men had wonderful ponies, and most of them had
themselves schooled the horses to the game. In those days not
even a millionaire duke could order three ready-made polo
ponies at a price that left very little change out of £1000.
Each one of the men who played had bought where he could
and taught the pony the game. We hear much and rightly
about the training of polo ponies and their condition, but
I doubt if more skill and patience and sound horsemanship
have ever been exercised on any of the crack ponies of our day
than were lavished on the early ponies, 'Fitz' and 'Nimble,'
wonderful old 'Piper,' 'Sister Sue,' and many more. But the
growth of polo was a silent one, for there were no daily
reports from the clubs, as there are now. A scanty paragraph
in the Field was all the notice the world had of the new game.
Mr Moray Brown was to come later, and the marvellous
influence his vivid pen had on the spread of the game has
never yet had quite justice done to it in the history of polo.

The name of Hurlingham and its polo spread far and wide.
Letters came from India, from America, from New Zealand,
and many other places. 'Tell us about polo and how to play it.
We have read your accounts, and it must be a splendid game.'
A New Zealand player has told me how the game won its way
among those hard-riding colonists in spite of the prejudice that
it was 'only a game for toffs.' Everywhere the game drew out
the necessary ponies. The great spread of polo is partly due
to the stimulus provided by the story of Hurlingham and its

play, the simple tale of its members' games from day to day, which filled about a third of Land and Water.

The game could not have failed to make its way in any case. But the management of Hurlingham, the skill of the early players, and the rise of Moray Brown, who more than any other has infused the fire of his own enthusiasm for sport into his writings, all combined to make the growth of polo in popular knowledge and estimation a rapid one. But I want to take my readers back to the days before Moray Brown, and to show how good the play was in the unrecorded times, when people still thought of Hurlingham chiefly as a place where they shot pigeons, and lost and won a good deal of money in so doing.

The fact was that long before Moray Brown wrote, the shooting had become a source of weakness rather than strength to the Club, and pigeons have long ceased to be shot there on the days fixed for great polo matches.

There can be no better way of tracing the growth of polo than by recalling some of the famous games that have been played on the Hurlingham ground. To begin with, let us take the Champion Cup of 1877, the first ever played for. For this six teams were entered – the Royal Horse Guards; the Staffordshire; the United Service Club; the International Gun and Polo Club, Brighton; the Tyros; the Monmouthshire. This was a strong entry. It was before the days when one team had established so great a superiority to all others that it was difficult to find clubs willing to compete for the cup. The play was fast throughout, and the final proved to be one of the most exciting games that have ever been played in the history of the cup. It was then still usual to have five men a-side and the International Gun and Polo Club seemed to have a great chance. Their team was Mr Arthur, Mr E. Kenyon Stow, Mr Howard, Mr J. E. Peat, and Mr A. E. Peat. Their opponents were – Monmouthshire: Captain F. Herbert, Mr Mellor, Mr R.

Herbert, Mr Hugh Owen, and Mr Edward Curre. Unluckily Mr Kenyon Stow was knocked over early in the game and had his leg broken. Thus the Brighton Club lost one of their best men. They played on, however, to the end, four against five. It is interesting to note that the Monmouthshire Club was not obliged to withdraw a man, and it also shows that the fifth man was an advantage. This, but for the fact that Monmouthshire won, we should in the light of our present knowledge have supposed not to be the case. Mr James Peat made a splendid fight for his side, and one of his runs foreshadowed his future fame. He gained possession of the ball and racing away was never stopped until he had scored a goal. This was on the Thursday, and on the Saturday we find the final tie sandwiched in between a *la crosse* match and a rose show. The Prince and Princess of Wales and the French, Danish, and Chinese Ambassadors came down. There were twenty-five coaches and a big gathering. The other club left in was the Tyros: Sir Bache Cunard, Mr A. de Murrietta, The Hon. C. C. Cavendish (now Major-General Lord Chesham), Mr C. de Murrietta, and Mr E. H. Baldock. The players rose to the occasion and the match was closely contested. When time was called neither side had scored a goal at all. There was a short rest and then the two teams ranged up again; but after playing for two additional quarters no goal had been struck, and the match was declared a draw. This is the only instance of a draw in the history of the Champion Cup, and the fact that no goal was made also stands by itself. Of the men who played in this match three became masters of hounds, Lord Chesham (the Bicester), Sir Bache Cunard (the Billesdon), Mr Reginald Herbert (the Monmouthshire). Lord Chesham served with great distinction in South Africa, where also Captain F. Herbert did good service. Mr Hugh Owen is starter to the Jockey Club.

Probably none of them have forgotten that desperate

struggle for the Champion Cup, which still lives in the memories of those who saw it, as one of the most exciting matches ever seen. Many years passed. The International Gun and Polo Club ceased to exist, and the Sussex team gradually established an ascendancy which was undisputed. When the Messrs. Peat were together they were invincible. The interest in the Champion Cup died down, and the Inter-Regimental Tournament became the chief event of the polo season. These matches, however, belong rather to Army polo than to Hurlingham, though to Captain Smythe is due the credit of organising them, and they have been played ever since, with the exception of the two years when the Boer War intervened, on the match ground at Hurlingham.

The Sussex team held the championship for seven years. The position of the brothers Peat was well deserved. They trained their own ponies and practised diligently. Their success was won by hard work, and Mr James Peat became the best forward of his day. Hurlingham has never seen a better player, and the picture of Mr 'Johnnie' Peat racing down the ground on 'Firefly' or 'Dynamite' no one who ever saw it will forget. 'Dynamite' was a great raking mare of the blood steeplechase-horse type. No one knows how she was bred, but she came, like many of our best ponies, from Ireland, and had probably no more than a nominal stain in her pedigree. She was not everyone's polo pony, and after about three minutes or so of fast play she caught hold of her bit in a way that might have disconcerted a less skilled horseman or more uncertain striker than her master. She never did play her best save for her master, and was a pony quite unsuited for a sticky game. But then no game was slow in which the famous pair took part. No player of the present day recalls Mr J. E. Peat, unless perhaps it is Mr A. Rawlinson when he is well on the ball.

But to return to the memorable match in 1894.

The Champion Cup had fallen to a low ebb. The Sussex County team had been victorious on seven occasions and had walked over twice (how do men walk over for a polo cup?), and there had been no contest at all in 1893. In 1894 there were but three entries, and the 4th Hussars had no real chance. It is probable, however, that they contributed to the victory of the Freebooters. The last-named had the luck to be drawn against them, and no doubt the game they were forced to play helped to put the Freebooters into their places. Captain Denis St George Daly was captain of the Freebooters and played back, a position in which he had in his best days few superiors. Captain Daly had arranged a first-rate team. Every man was exactly in his right position, and was riding ponies that suited him and that were well fitted for the place they occupied. Mr Hardy had two ponies 'Elastic' and 'Blackman,' the former one of the very best No. 1 ponies that I have ever seen. She had a rare turn of speed, could start at a touch, and was as quick into her stride as pony can be.

Lord Southampton rode 'Lady Day,' the wonderful chestnut with a white stocking. This pony combined pace and stamina with smoothness of action that made riding her a pleasure. Later she passed into the possession of the Royal Horse Guards team. She was one of the best heavy-weight No. 2 ponies of her day. Captain Le Gallais rode the Arab 'Johnnie,' a dark chestnut, 'White Rose,' a beautiful high-caste horse, and Mr G. Hardy's 'Sailor,' somewhat later to be sold for the highest price ever paid for a polo pony. Probably he made his name on this memorable occasion. 'Sailor' is still playing, and is as handy a pony as ever he was.

Captain Daly was at that time the owner of two as good ponies as any man need wish to own. 'Wig' was the steadiest, 'Skittles' could all but fly. The third, 'Martingale,' though not equal to the other two and not too easy to ride, did well in his owner's hands. The team of ponies that the

Peat brothers and Lord Harrington brought out were a living epitome of the history of polo. There they were all looking as fit and well as one of the best polo grooms in England could make them. All bought and schooled by their owners, they had played in every first-class match. 'Firefly,' 'Dynamite,' 'Piper,' 'Edge,' 'Sister Sue,' 'Seagull,' 'Nimble.' Of these 'Piper' and 'Seagull' were perhaps actually the best, though 'Dynamite' chiefly caught the public eye and the fancy of the spectators. Lord Harrington had the chestnut 'The Girl,' 'Arthur Roberts,' and one-eyed 'Cyclops,' the last named a polo pony, hack, and cubhunter, and good for all. A trifle over the regulation height he was, but in those days we were not so particular. The height was 14.1 it is true, but if you could not find a pony to suit you of that height you did the best you could. No one grumbled, or if they did nobody paid any attention.

All Messrs Peat's ponies were sold not long after at Tattersall's, and 'Dynamite' and 'Nimble' (bought by Mr W. H. Walker) went for 960 guineas the pair, by far the largest price ever paid for polo ponies up to that time. 'Sailor' – he played in the same match – was destined, as we know, to beat the record in price. It was the opinion of a sound judge who looked over the ponies before the match that they were the best lot in the world, and he was probably right. We have many first-rate ponies now, but I doubt if for playing qualities we could beat the Champion Cup team of 1894. The Sussex were the favourites of course. Indeed, though there is not much betting at polo, I think an observant person might have taken a few friendly wagers at eight or ten to one against the Freebooters. It was well known that Mr Arthur Peat had but recently recovered from a severe illness and it was obvious to anyone that he was not himself. Lord Harrington and Mr A. E. Peat were on the season's form certainly not better than Lord Southampton and Captain Le Gallais. So that the sides were in reality fairly well matched.

Yet in those days we could see nothing but Mr J. E. Peat, and had come to believe, not without reason, that every side on which he played must therefore be victorious. Looking back – and it is always so easy to be wise after the event – we can see plainly that the Freebooters were the better balanced team. This game was in fact one of the first great struggles between combination and individual brilliancy.

At first it looked like an easy victory for Sussex. Twice Mr J. Peat scored. The first goal he hit, and dropping on the ball, no one knew whence, he sat down on 'Firefly' and in two splendid strokes scored. Once more he won the goal, and in this we may note he showed what a fine player he was. He was galloping with the ball, but Captain Daly, strong, steady, and not to be slipped again, was in the right place for a backhander. There was one chance and Mr Peat took it. Calling to Lord Harrington to take the ball he hurled himself on Captain Daly, and gave his 2 and 3 a clear run for the goal, of which they availed themselves. Thus it was that Sussex justified their backers, and at the close of the first quarter of an hour the score was Sussex two, Freebooters nil.

Fast play along the boards.

There was a desperate struggle later in the game. Captain Daly played as he had never played before. Lord Southampton was in one of his hitting moods when nothing seemed to stop him, and Captain Le Gallais was, as always, a brilliant polo player. On the other hand, Mr J. Peat was everywhere and always effective. That the Freebooters had the best of a struggle which for eagerness has never been surpassed was shown by the fact that at the close of the third quarter (this game was played in fifteen minute periods) the score was two all.

Sussex might, we could now see, be beaten, but we opened our eyes when, early in the last period, we saw Mr Peat on 'Dynamite' gallop away with the ball, having indeed a start of a length in his favour. Captain Le Gallais on 'Sailor' was pressing in hot pursuit. The brown pony laid himself down to his work. He was actually overhauling the mare. He ranged alongside, and one of the finest horsemen in India actually rode off the Sussex No. 1. Could we believe our eyes? This fired the Freebooters, and though the ball was behind and Captain Daly had to hit out, he made one of the finest strokes of his polo career. In a polo game as in war you cannot win unless you will take risks. Captain Daly hit right across his own goal to Captain Le Gallais who galloped away with the ball hitting on near or offside – he could not miss till just at the end a twist caused the ball to get out of his reach, but Mr Gerald Hardy, steadiest of players, was behind and struck it through the goal posts, and his too was the hand that scored the final goal that enabled the Freebooters to win by four goals to three.

I have dwelt on this match because none was ever so important to the future of polo as this. It marked the close of the first period of the history of English polo, and was destined to give the game a wider range. One club, one ground, one team were no longer to suffice. It was the coming of age of the game that had been begun on Mr Naylor's orchard just twenty years before.

The Sussex team, and to a great extent the old Hurlingham, passed away, and there is a danger lest men should forget what horsemen and players they were, what they did for the game, and what a tradition of fair-play they have left to those who come after them. But polo was much too full of life to stand still, and, as Mr Moray Brown said at the time, the result did 'incalculable good to polo in general,' in so far as it showed that neither skill nor ponies could ensure a permanent superiority to any team. The Sussex were no longer the only team, and Hurlingham was no longer the only ground. In that year 1894 the Ranelagh Club had changed hands, and was already started on the progress.

But there is yet a third great match which must not be passed over when telling the story of the Hurlingham Club. This was again the marking off of a new development of the game. The Rugby Club on 12th June 1897 won the Champion Cup with a team that showed combination and brilliancy together. There has never been a finer back player than the late Mr W. J. Drybrough. A most powerful horseman, he was a hard striker, and his near-side backhanders were marvellous for accuracy and force. Captain Renton, the Rugby No. 2, was and is a beautiful player. He is a fine horseman and his style of riding and of play are the perfection of finish and ease. To see Captain Renton at his best was an object lesson in polo. An excellent back, as he proved when, in the 17th Lancers, he played No. 4 for his regimental team, he was even better as No. 2 in the Rugby team. Captain Miller and his brother Mr G. A. Miller were business-like players as always, whose interest in polo has never flagged and whose knowledge of the game is never at fault.

The Freebooters had Mr Hardy, Mr A. Rawlinson, Mr W. Buckmaster, and Mr John Watson. This was Mr Buckmaster's first appearance in a Champion Cup. The Freebooters looked like a very strong team, but lacked the combining power of the winning team of 1894. Although that team had not played very often together, yet Captain Daly and Captain Le Gallais had both had experience in regimental polo which enabled them to fit into any team. Like its predecessor, the game was played in glorious weather, and it excited scarcely less interest. For fifty-five minutes the result hung in the balance. It was not until the fourth ten minutes that the Freebooters began to show signs of giving way. Rugby seemed to gain confidence and pace as the game went on, and the Freebooters were obviously struggling to avoid defeat. At forty minutes neither side had scored, but the tactics of Rugby, particularly those of Mr E. D. Miller, who did all he could to make opportunities for Captain Renton, were beginning to tell. So fine and effective was the defence of both sides that though each side pressed in turn there was no score for fifty-five minutes. In the last three minutes Captain Renton scored twice, and the Rugby team won the cup, which they have held, with the exception of 1900 and 1904, when the Old Cantabs won it. But they have never since had quite so perfect a team. I well remember shortly after the match Mr W. J. Drybrough saying to me that never again would Rugby have such a team, a remark which received a sad confirmation when one of the finest 'backs' of modern polo passed away from us not many weeks afterwards.

Thus we have brought the history of Hurlingham, which is for twenty-three years the story of polo in England, down to the present time. We have seen how at that Club polo first took form, and from an aimless scramble gradually rose to be a game of skill. The three matches we have sketched show how the game developed until we arrive at the present game of combination. The side, which consisted of four men more or less fitted into each other's play, has now become under the Rugby system, as it were, a single body moved by a single will. Something of this was no doubt learned from such teams as the 13th Hussars and the Durham Light Infantry. The pony, which in the first stages had been merely a conveyance, has now become a highly trained and perfected instrument of the player. The placing of the ball for one's own side is now more important than any other stroke. The ball was originally delivered in the direction of the goal and the rest left to chance. I well remember how we used to hit as hard as we could and gallop as fast as we were able in pursuit. Now the main object is to pass or place the ball. A first-rate side may and often does obtain possession of the ball, and by dexterous passing from one to the other actually prevent the opponents from touching it till it is struck triumphantly through the posts. Every change in the style of play has been tested in the Champion Cup, and each of the most notable victories has marked an improvement which has been made in the play. Mr Peat and Mr Kenyon Stow taught us to sit down in the saddle and strike with a straight arm. Mr John Watson showed us what the backhander could do, and how the No. 4 should not only keep his goal but turn defence into attack, so that when he had successfully driven the ball from his own goal he was also preparing for an attack on that of his opponents. Lastly, we have learned by combination how the best can be made of the moderate player. Thus, although the importance of the really first-rate man is as great as ever, the present style of play enables more to be made of the average player, and a well-directed team of mediocrities will have its share of success.

But the success of Hurlingham in establishing and improving the game has not been of unmixed benefit to the Club. There is one thing the original promoters of Hurlingham polo could not, and did not, foresee – the immense expansion of the game. The development of the Club is restricted by the inexorable limits of space. Hurlingham rules and the Polo Committee have more influence than ever, but apart from its associations the Club is one among several competing for the favour of polo players. The quality of its polo is as high as ever, but the quantity is, by no fault of the Club, deficient. The splendid members' games which were so good to watch have passed away with the men who made them what they were. Ten matches are now played in a week. Two were enough in the old days. And Hurlingham in 1904 put forward a programme of sixty-four matches.

But if the Hurlingham Club has lost, as it was inevitable it should lose, its singular position as the only polo club in London, so long as it continues to make rules for the game, so long will it be the first polo club in the world.

Recent changes have altered the position of Hurlingham. The old Polo Committee did excellent service. The General Committee of the Club nominated the best players and the men of most influence in the game. This Polo Committee met seldom and moved but slowly in the direction of change. Mr Watson's wise dictum that it is much better to leave polo alone than to spoil it by over-legislation, was always before the minds of the Committee. We have already seen under what a very simple code the game flourished. The Hurlingham Polo Committee, though, moved slowly, yet surely, and each change as it came was an improvement, rendered necessary by the altered conditions of the game. A more scientific game requires stricter and more definite rules.

In 1897 the County Polo Association was founded and at once assumed a kind of intermediate direction and guidance of county clubs. Then in 1902 Hurlingham widened the constitution of its Polo Committee, accepted three representative members from the County Polo Association, two from the Army Committee, and one from Roehampton. This representation is weighted by the condition that the members sent from these various bodies must be members of Hurlingham. The voting power still remains with Hurlingham. That club can outvote all the representatives combined; even if Ranelagh had sent the number they were invited to. This they did not care to do, having a strong polo committee of their own. The new Hurlingham Committee, although it is a rather anomalous body, performing public functions after the fashion of a private Club Committee, may nevertheless work well enough in practice until we are ripe for a national association. Yet those of us who knew the game in its earlier days may be forgiven if we look back with regret, which is not altogether sentimental, on the old Hurlingham Committee, which had no love for change for the sake of change. At all events we shall not forget the debt of gratitude polo players owe to the earlier Committee and the men who, like Mr John Watson, Lord Harrington, Mr Gerald Hardy, Mr A. Rawlinson, Captain St G. Daly and Sir Walter Smythe, helped to rule the fortunes of the game, and guided its developments, on the whole wisely and well, through the difficult years of its beginnings.

3
The Ranelagh Club and the Expansion of Polo

The want of space at Hurlingham was felt very early in the history of the game. But two circumstances prevented that Club from extending its limits, the feeling that polo was possibly only a passing fashion, and a certain unwillingness on the part of the pigeon-shooting members to be swamped by the polo players.

Among the early polo players there were none better than the two brothers Herbert. Captain, now Major F. Herbert, was playing only the other day. He was when I first saw him, a very fine player indeed, and a good horseman. Mr Reginald Herbert of Clytha I never saw at polo, as he had retired from first-class matches before my return to England, but he was one of those who were often included in tournaments, and he had a sound knowledge of the game. Mr Herbert, with the assistance of his brother and of Mr Kenyon Stow, determined to supply the need for more polo. There was in that year a house and grounds to let which had belonged to the father of the last Lord Ranelagh. This place had been used as a club already. It was close to Hurlingham, a matter of some moment, since polo players in those days were limited in number. It seemed likely that, if the two clubs were close together, the members would pass from one to the other. This was what happened, and as the Ranelagh Club laid itself out for pony racing, in which Mr Herbert and his brother were interested, and for which Hurlingham had no space available, the new club was at once successful. The house was a fine one of the comfortable Georgian type, of which the last occupant had been Mr Johnston, the proprietor of the *Standard*. The idea of the founders of Ranelagh was to establish a social club on the lines of Hurlingham.

The year 1878 was that of its opening. The Club had a strong Committee, which included such names as the late Duke of Beaufort, Lord Hartington, now Duke of Devonshire, Mr Cavendish, now Lord Chesham, Mr Henry Chaplin, Lords Shrewsbury and Valentia. Lord Shrewsbury is still a member of the Committee of the existing Ranelagh Club, and Lord Valentia is Chairman of the Hurlingham Polo Committee. The Club seems to have been a pleasant resort. Lawn tennis tournaments were made rather a feature, and pony shows and pony racing drew considerable crowds. The first notable polo match was one played by electric light, at which the Prince of Wales (King Edward VII), the King of Greece, and other distinguished personages were present. The whole affair seems to have been a great success, and may have done something to popularise the game. At all events the presence of the Prince of Wales stamped polo with the approval of the world of fashion. It will be noted that the sides now consisted of four players: Hurlingham – Lord Petersham, better known to polo players of today as the Earl of Harrington, Mr J. Peat, Mr Wyndham Quin, Mr E. Peat, a very strong side; Ranelagh – Mr A. Peat, Lord Lewes, Mr Anderton, and Mr E. H. Baldock.

The reporter in his admiration of the Chinese lanterns that were hung about the grounds has entirely forgotten to tell us about the game, which, in spite of the well-arranged sides, was probably of no great account. That there was a special ball, large and light, manufactured for the occasion and the band played the 'Lost Chord' during the match, is about the extent of our information.

This fete gave a start to Ranelagh, and shows incidentally that people did not take their polo so seriously then as we do now. The Ranelagh of that day was in no sense a rival of Hurlingham. It was scarcely a separate club. To pass from one to the other was but a step, and since Hurlingham could not accommodate more than a part of the members who

Ranelagh Club house.

Ranelagh polo pavilion on the old ground.

desired to belong to it, people found Ranelagh a pleasant alternative. In the meantime, the opening of the new club was a sign of the progress of polo and the cause of further expansion. The game was played every day except Sundays on one or other of the two grounds. The Ranelagh Club had not, however, at this time a sufficiently long lease to give it the necessary condition of permanence, and Mr Herbert had to look about for another suitable place. The speculative builder had already marked the Ranelagh House of that day for his own. Now, on the site of the club house and polo ground are rows of smug villas and blocks of flats.

But there could be no doubt as to the suitability of the next site chosen. Barn Elms was vacant. It would be difficult to imagine a place more fitted for a club. The property was a part of the old estate belonging to the Dean and Chapter of St Paul's, and was therefore in the hands of the Ecclesiastical Commissioners. The house, gardens, and park, which were of a delightful old-world character, covered about one hundred acres. Had Barn Elms been designed as a polo club it could hardly have been better planned. The beauty of the surroundings and the fact that though barely a mile from Hammersmith Bridge and less from Putney it is a perfect country house, give it a special charm. The grounds have two entrances, one opposite to the village of Barnes and the other close to Putney Common. Nor is this all, for the Club can never be built out; it is bounded on one side by Barnes Common and on another by the reservoir of the Waterworks, while there is a charming river front separated and protected by a wide stream from the towing path. So rural is the district that within the memory of men now living woodcock and snipe have been shot there, and even as late as 1894, when I was manager of the Club, I have seen rabbits and pheasants in the shrubberies in the quiet hours before the members began to arrive. The grounds are a paradise for birds. In 1895 one of the sights of the season was a tiny blue tit which had built its nest close to the nozzle by which the watering hose were connected with the hydrant. The little bird sat there undisturbed by the fixing or unfixing of the pipes, the tramp of the crowds on the lawn, or the sounds of the Hungarian band, which was stationed near the spot. But this is anticipating, for at first of course there were small beginnings. One polo ground sufficed, and a race-course for ponies was laid out. The club-house was fitted up simply but comfortably.

When Mr Herbert decided to give up the management in 1894, the Club fell into the hands of men who could see not only its advantages, but could look forward to its future expansion. These men were Dr George Hastings, Mr James Leslie Wanklyn, M.P. for Bradford, and Mr Charles Lewinger, and later Lord Ava and Sir Stanley Clarke. To Dr Hastings are due chiefly the growth and success of the Club. Nothing less than perfection would satisfy him. In details he was as thorough as in larger matters he took wide views. No one has ever worked harder himself or been the cause of more work in others. He caused some opposition, but he was generally right, and those who differed most from him at first have often come to see the wisdom of his action. Dr. Hastings was hard on his workers, as it seemed to them, but he was always loyal in supporting them, and gradually won the confidence and esteem of them all. The Committee of the Club was a strong one, with the Earl of Dudley as chairman. The fact remains that the Club has prospered steadily, and holds a high place not only as a polo club, but for its golf, croquet, and lawn tennis. The golf, for which Mr Wanklyn did a good deal, was even more important than the polo at first. My late friend Mr Adams, the secretary for golf, was universally liked. The first secretary was Mr G. A. Williams, and he is there still, and the first polo manager was Mr Moray Brown, with the present writer as his unofficial assistant, and eventually as his successor.

It was an interesting but anxious time. Yet there were few set-backs. There was another point in the Club's favour which might easily have escaped some men, but was fully valued by the new Committee, and their chairman Lord Dudley, to whom the Club owes much of its prosperity. Under their care the historical associations of the Club with the Kitcat Club were cherished, and commemorated in the design for the Club's note-paper, by the portraits on the walls, and the style of decoration in the house.

The first thing to be done, if the Club was to take its place in the polo world as one of the chief centres of the game, was to improve the grounds. You cannot make a polo ground all at once. It is a matter of labour and of time. From the first hour when I went down with Mr Moray Brown and we tried to devise a means of widening the existing match ground, the polo grounds were never out of our minds. The Ranelagh ground was not then what it is now, the best in London. Parts have been taken up and re-laid, hillocks have been removed, the boundary boards twice placed at a greater width apart. From one end of the year to the other the polo ground is a source of anxiety, the object of constant care. Then the new ground was made, and I can never watch polo on it without thinking of the anxieties of those early days, when the far side after being carefully laid began to sink and become boggy and deep. The polo players were a pleasant set, but still they always felt, not perhaps unjustly, that if the ground was not right the polo manager must somehow be in fault.

Then there were the golf players, a delightful set of men. But if golf players have a fault it is that they take themselves so seriously. Now at Ranelagh the golf players thought that they were in some danger of being put on one side for the polo, and the new ground was near some of their beautifully kept greens. So near in fact that it was said that the first day polo was played on the new ground, an enthusiastic golfer sat in the middle of a green to protect it from sacrilegious hoofs. But we did in fact take every care of the golfers' interests, and they came to see it and gave us a hearty support at last. Still it was an anxious time, for the Club was still in the making. Then, too, from Dr. Hastings' designs we built a row of boxes. We wondered if thirty would be needed. That was not ten years ago; now 200 boxes are not enough to satisfy the wants of members. In the early days we were feeling our way, and the Committee began to make the Saturday afternoons as attractive as possible. The entertainments were, and are successful. The first polo gymkhana was almost too successful, for provision was made for tea for 500 people, and 1500 came down, and the tea and cake, which were so important a feature, gave out. Our polo was good, and a band of keen players made the Club their headquarters. Some of them, Captain Greville, 1st Life Guards, and Mr E. T. Hohler, his brother, and Mr W. H. Walker, have retired from the game; Major Victor Ferguson, Captain Rose of the R. H. G., and Mr A. M. Knowles all met soldiers' deaths. But many of the old players are still in the first rank, Mr E. B. Sheppard, Lord Shrewsbury, Captain Heseltine. Every year something has been done to add to the convenience of polo players. In 1896 Captain Miller and Mr George Miller succeeded to the management of the polo, while Lord Ava became the general manager of the Club, and afterwards one of the directors. The Ranelagh Club has been a great factor in the expansion of polo.

The Committee have had the interests of the game at heart, and have spared neither money nor labour to give opportunities to players and comfort to spectators. It is not too much to say that when Ranelagh was reopened in 1894, the future of polo hung in the balance. Hurlingham with all its advantages was limited in the matter of space. Men who keep three or four ponies wish to have as much polo as possible. But Hurlingham had then but one ground, and this was scarcely enough for the existing players, and the younger players had but a small chance of practice. When therefore the two grounds at Ranelagh were opened the opportunity was eagerly seized on. Many of the members of Hurlingham joined the Club, and in a very short time there were plenty of players at both.

Recruits flowed in rapidly to the game, and new matches and tournaments were arranged and the entry lists filled at once. By the third season Ranelagh was full to overflowing with eager candidates for polo. The grounds were improved. The old ground was re-laid, the new one enlarged, stabling was built, and the boxes engaged before the paint was dry on the doors. Then came the building of the pavilion, which has twice been enlarged and improved since. I have given a plan of this building among the illustrations of this book, because the Ranelagh pavilion is without any question the most convenient building- for its purpose in existence.

This pavilion was not, however, a mere luxury – it has had a great effect on the popularity of polo in London. A game is indeed first of all for the players, but spectators too count for much in the prosperity of cricket, football, and polo.

The taste for looking on at polo had to be created, and the Ranelagh pavilion, with its tea-rooms and its comforts, owes its success not so much to these luxurious additions as to the fact that it is by far the best place in London to see a match from. First-class polo, if it is a genuine contest and not a mere exhibition game, is most attractive as a spectacle. Whereas, at first, the other entertainments provided drew away the bulk of the spectators, a really fine polo match is today sure of a large and understanding crowd of lookers-on. The next step was to rebuild the pavilion on the New ground, and then came one of the greatest triumphs of the management – the construction of the third ground and a practice ground and the building of a third pavilion with a terrace promenade in front. This last ground was no easy matter, for there was, across the Beverley Brook, a swampy though picturesque stretch of ground. This had to be re-laid with firm soil, and tons of the earth excavated from Walsingham House and the tube railways were carted up to the Club and laid on the surface. The result is a polo ground, which appears on the plan perfectly level, and is already covered with a carpet of sound turf.

Thus, since Ranelagh was opened, polo has indeed grown. The Club has trebled its opportunities for play, more than quadrupled its accommodation for ponies. As to the opportunities, there were in 1904 eight tournaments: the opening handicap, the Hunt Challenge Cup, the Army Cup, the Open Cup (one of the great polo events of the year), the Aldershot Cup (of which more hereafter), the Novices' Cup, the Subalterns' Cup, and the Hunt tournament. Altogether a total of in matches were played, the largest number yet played at one club in any polo season.

The services of Ranelagh to polo were marked during the year 1904 by two daring but successful innovations. I refer to the Aldershot Cup, which is a one-day tournament. Soldiers' polo nowadays must neither take up too much time nor require the expenditure of too much money, and the Ranelagh Committee in instituting a cup which could be played for in a single day, thus showing the possibility of short matches, no doubt did a considerable service. I have always contended that one way to reduce the expenditure on polo is to shorten the time of play. The present sixty minutes is too much for all except the best ponies, and much too long for lookers-on except in those games where the best style of play is to be seen.

The other step forward was the formation of a club team. While such combinations as Handley Cross, the Magpies, the Freebooters, and others, give us excellent polo, there is not the same interest attaching to their success or failure as there is to a regimental team, or one representative of a club or, like the Old Cantabs, of a university. It is one of the promising signs of polo that club teams are each year more in evidence. Rugby and the Old Cantabs have been hitherto the only teams to which this special kind of interest has attached, outside the regimental teams. Now Ranelagh has a team to represent it, and the followers of the red and white had a new interest in the season. A most successful attempt it was, and the team – Captain L. C. D. Jenner, Mr A. Rawlinson, Mr F. A. Gill, and Mr Scott Robson – well upheld the honour of the Club.

The success of Ranelagh has thus led to a great expansion of the game, and when Roehampton (of which I have yet to write) was started as a result of the demand for more polo, no difference was noted in the Ranelagh Club gatherings; indeed the latter Club has had to exclude from all except the open tournaments players who are not members of the Club.

That polo exists at all is due to Hurlingham, that it holds the place it does is the result of the enterprising and successful conduct of the game at Ranelagh during the last ten years. Had the Ranelagh Club been closed when Mr Herbert wished to retire, polo would not have had the position either in London or the country which it holds to-day. While the attractions of the Club as a social resort have been acknowledged everywhere, its serious side and its great services to the game have been somewhat overlooked.

Every game has, at its beginning, a tendency to fall into the hands of a small circle of skilful players, and thus to discourage the beginner. This danger has loomed large in the case of polo. Ranelagh has always so managed the game as to give to all members of the Club, so far as may be, equal rights. Their Polo Committee, a very strong and representative body, has taken a wide view on most subjects connected with the game.

Every member is sure of his share of play, and certain to be placed in a match in which his powers of play will be exercised and tested. The convenience of Ranelagh, of course, and that it is the best-equipped and most comfortable of social clubs, are advantages which are, so to speak, thrown in for the polo player. The historic associations, the fact that it was the first club founded for the express purpose of playing polo, its twenty-six years (1878–1904) of growth, the many distinguished players who have used its grounds, as well as the unrivalled beauty of the place itself, make it regarded by its older members with an affection and loyalty something akin to one's feeling for one's regiment or university, and based on the same associations of history and comradeship.

But now to turn to particular matches, we find that Ranelagh provides us with some notable games, each of which marks an advance in the game of polo. In 1899, on May 27, was played the final of the Hunt Cup. This is a challenge cup open to all members of hunts, provided they have subscribed £20 to the funds of the hunt, and followed the pack on at least ten occasions. Two Hunts, the Pytchley and the Warwickshire, were marked out for this cup.

Both hunts have clubs within reach of their members, the Rugby ground, though actually in the Warwickshire country, being convenient for Pytchley men, while the Warwickshire Polo Club at Sydenham Farm, Leamington, is a leading county club. The sides were: Pytchley – Mr C. Nickalls, Captain Renton (Hon. Secretary of the hunt), Mr Walter Buckmaster, and Mr P. W. Nickalls; Warwickshire – Mr F. Hargreaves, Mr F. J. Mackey, Mr F. Freake, and Mr W. J. Drybrough. So evenly matched were the teams that at first both were on the defensive. Like two boxers sparring for an opening, they hit and countered, and the play was more careful than dashing. Mr W. J. Drybrough was in his best form. It was from one of his well-placed backhanders that Warwickshire was enabled to make the first serious attack.

They just failed to score, but they held the Pytchley to their goal. Mr P. Nickalls, always a fine player, though without the experience of the game that has now, defended well, and Mr Buckmaster was everywhere. Yet at length the ball shot out of a scrimmage and through the posts. Then the attacks from either side grew more and more fierce, as each in turn failed to break down the defence of their adversaries. It was in fact one of the finest games of defence that was ever seen. There was but one umpire, Mr G. A. Miller, and he was only once or twice called upon to intervene. But as the game went on the Pytchley men improved. Mr C. Nickalls as No. 1, who had in the earlier stages been somewhat baffled by Mr Drybrough, particularly when that player was riding the white-faced chestnut 'Charlton,' probably one of the best No. 4 ponies that ever played in a game, improved as he went on. The goals came but slowly, and one all was the score up to within three short minutes of the last bell. Then Warwickshire, admirably mounted, were seen to be stretching away towards the goal at the Hammersmith end. At the moment when victory seemed within their grasp Mr Patteson Nickalls hit a masterly backhander, then shouted to Mr Buckmaster to take it, and like one man the Pytchley team came round for a combined rush. Defence had become attack. Mr Buckmaster had possession, near side or off side were the same to him till chancing on some rough ground the ball twisted and bumped, but Captain Renton was there and with one of the neatest of wrist strokes made an angle shot and hit the ball through. As it rolled between the posts the bell rang, and the Pytchley Hunt were victorious.

The Hunt Cup was, owing to this and other notable matches to which it has given occasion, the first of the Ranelagh tournaments to attract notice, but the same year the Open Cup final was one of the most interesting games of the season. In this tournament the challengers play off the ties, the winners meeting the holders of the cup in the final. Although this apparently gives an advantage to the holders, yet this Cup has changed hands as often as any. It generally comes late in the season, when there are few matches of the first importance left undecided, and the players are in their very best form. There is probably no match of the season which is a more perfect example of scientific polo. If a critic of the game wishes to see the state of polo in any one year, let him follow carefully the first-class teams in the Ranelagh Open Cup.

But in recent days no matches have excited so much interest and excitement as the three played by Ranelagh teams against the American players. Of these men and their skill I have written elsewhere in this book. Two of the games of which I write were friendly matches. The wet ground on the first two days seemed to suit the Americans. I had on both occasions looked over the ponies and, putting aside one or two, they were not equal in make and shape to the class of pony which is usually seen at Ranelagh. But in practice they proved to be able to turn quickly and spring sharply into their stride in a way that made them, on a wet day and with the ground cut up, quite able to hold their own. The Americans won both matches, showing a remarkable aptitude in adapting themselves to our English rules of offside and stick-crooking. The brothers Waterbury had never been in England before, but they had played with Mr Kenyon Stow in America, who was one of the best of the early players of the game. These were some of the few games in which both brothers Waterbury played during the visit of the American team.

This was Mr Gill's first season of management, and he was at once wise in securing, and fortunate in having the opportunity to arrange, these matches. We shall not easily forget the first match. The rain poured down during the whole game. It was played on the new ground on which the recently built pavilion was being used for the first time. But, rain or fine, everyone wanted to see the Americans, and every inch of shelter was occupied. Those who wished to watch the play closely had perforce to stand out in the rain. Yet in the excitement of the match that followed everything was forgotten except the interest of the moment. The American team were Messrs Cowdin, Mr M. Waterbury, Mr Agassiz, and Mr L. Waterbury. Their opponents were called the Old Cantabs, but as a matter of fact there were but two of that team among them. Mr W. M'Creery (from California), Mr C. Nickalls, Oxford, Mr W. Buckmaster, and Mr C. D. Miller made up the team. The impression that remained, when at last the Americans won, was that they were too quick for our men. They were in fact, on the day, the better team. Mr L. Waterbury's defence was very strong indeed, and Mr M. Waterbury's attack very dashing, while sounder players in a fast game than Mr Agassiz and Mr Cowdin no one would wish to see.

The combination, or perhaps the confidence, of the English team was not good. The men did not suit each other's play. Profiting by the lessons of defeat, Mr Gill on the next occasion strengthened his team, which now consisted of Mr F. M. Freake, Mr F. Gill, Mr W. Buckmaster, and Mr P. Nickalls.

The Americans put Mr Agassiz, a player who raised his reputation very much by the style of his play in England, as No. 1, Mr 'Monty' Waterbury No. 2, Mr Foxhall Keane, No. 3, and Mr L. Waterbury 'back'. At first Ranelagh had the better of the struggle. Mr Freake, who combined hard and strong hitting with a fast pony, made several fine runs and scored a goal for his side. The two Waterburys then seemed to improve as though by magic, and we realised how good they were. They made a splendid goal by combined play. When we recollect that in America the grounds are much harder than with us, and that the absence of offside and stick-crooking throws open the goal to hard riding and hard hitting, their adaptation to the new conditions was little short of wonderful, and stamped the two brothers as first-class players, according to the English standard.

I believe our American visitors were much struck by a goal which Mr Buckmaster backhanded in his peculiarly graceful style. Nevertheless the Americans steadily gained the upper hand, and made two goals in quick succession. Once more Mr Freake, in brilliant style, galloped out with the ball, and, never touched or hindered and seemingly quite unhampered by the ground, which by this time was somewhat cut up, made a splendid goal. In the end the American team won by five goals to three. This was perhaps their high-water mark, and I think no one who saw the matches in the International tournament will consider that they quite equalled the form shown on this occasion. It was evident that the Ranelagh ground suited their play.

There was another memorable event at Ranelagh when the American visitors played a match before their Majesties the King and Queen, and the Prince and Princess Charles of Denmark. There were, it is said, more than five thousand people present. Certainly the Club was very full, although the space at Ranelagh enables a large number of people to see the game. It was a great struggle, and fought out with pluck to the very end. The Americans again altered their arrangement, the brothers Waterbury being 1 and 4 respectively, and Mr Cowdin and Mr Foxhall Keane 2 and 3. This enabled these old friends and polo partners to be together, and as they thoroughly understood one another's play the team was strengthened thereby. The Ranelagh team was a strong one – Captain L. C. D. Jenner, Mr Rawlinson, Mr Gill, and Mr Scott-Robson. The last named is a fine player from South America, with the rare gift of being able to play with either the right or left hand. He is a fine horseman and a hard hitter, rather handicapped by his weight. Another point of interest to polo players is that both the present polo managers of Ranelagh were in the game. Captain Jenner snatched the ball and raced away to the goal. Mr Gill rode hard and worked hard, and he and Mr Rawlinson combined well in attack. The last named is a tower of strength to any side if he can attack, and Ranelagh led at half-time by one goal. Mr M. Waterbury made a splendid long shot at about this period of the game, and he is evidently an adherent of the sound polo maxim that when the goal-posts are open it is wise to try for a long shot. It was an exciting struggle, and the score was four all, and but three minutes remained. Ranelagh pressed, and Captain Jenner, who had scored the first goal of the match, also hit the last and winning stroke. Thus the Ranelagh Club was able to show to one of the largest gatherings of the season one of the most exciting matches in the memorable Coronation year.

The Ranelagh Club, which was the first London social club for the express purpose of the game of polo, is now the largest in the world. It has three polo grounds and a most comfortable and luxurious club-house. The financial success of the Club has enabled the managers to expend large sums (more than £30,000) on improvements, without borrowing. The men who supplied the original capital have been content with a modest five per cent. I do not think that anyone who visits Ranelagh for the first time as it is now will accuse me of exaggeration if I say that it is quite the best equipped and best managed club of its kind in the world. The situation is incomparable, the beauty of the grounds, the old-world character of the house, which has not been spoiled by the additions made to it, give a charm to the Club, and make it one of the most notable resorts that fashion has ever had. Ranelagh on Saturday afternoons when some great polo matches are to be played – the final of the Army Cup, the Hunt Cup, the Open Cup, or the Novices, or when Royalty is there – is one of the most brilliant sights in the world, and certainly one which no foreign visitor should miss if he wishes to see English society at play, and polo at its best.

4

The Growth of Polo in London & the Provinces

The development of polo, after the reconstruction of the Ranelagh Club in 1894, was so rapid that the demand for time and space for play was quite beyond the power of Hurlingham and Ranelagh to satisfy. For a short time the Wimbledon Club had a considerable success. Its grounds were well laid out and the class of polo played was excellent. But Wimbledon had one disadvantage to contend with – it was too far away from London, and society would not drive the extra distance or travel in crowded trains on a Saturday afternoon. So in spite of a polo management that was as good as any we have seen, and a ground that a few years' care would have made delightful to play on, Wimbledon ceased to exist as a club and the ground is now used by the Household Brigade as a private polo ground. Thus the failure of Wimbledon and the success of Ranelagh alike opened the way for a new club. The Grove House estate at Roehampton was available, and the Roehampton Club was started. Captain Miller, the manager, had had much experience. The Rugby Club had been practically founded by him. He had made the annual tournament of that Club one of the events of the autumn polo season, and he had learned, with the assistance of Mr G. A. Miller, during a successful polo managership at Ranelagh, how to conduct a London club. The Rugby team were Champion Cup winners, and the most skilled in a close yet flexible combination. The team which played for Rugby in 1897 was one of the best civilian polo teams seen in our time. Roehampton was founded and started into existence full grown, with three polo grounds, a comfortable pavilion, and water laid on to all the grounds. The Club has a charming situation between Roehampton lane and Priory lane, and the founders were fortunate in securing a seven years' lease, and earned our gratitude by keeping at bay the builder, to whom its three frontages must be an immense temptation. Roehampton has no club-house, but the pavilion is well arranged, with luncheon and tea-rooms and a drawing-room for lady visitors. Some of the Household Cavalry established their regimental games there, and a good programme of tournaments was started. The first season was marked by some admirable games and matches, and in spite of great disadvantages (it was the Coronation year, the American teams were playing their international matches, and the weather was as bad as it could be) the club grew. The last two seasons have been better, and Roehampton has had time to develop, and by 1904 the club had a strong and representative team who are at present the holders of the Ranelagh Open Cup, beating the winners of the Champion Cup of 1904. It is true the Old Cantabs were out of form, but with Rugby not up to their full strength, Roehampton was the best team. Much good polo is played on the Roehampton grounds, but there has never perhaps been any match to excel in interest two which were played in the Inauguration Cup. The former was the first match on English ground in which the Americans were defeated; the latter was one of the closest games ever fought. It was drawn at last, for one of the Rugby men met with a serious accident. I take the account from the excellent report given in the Field of 17th May 1902. The Americans were represented by Mr T. Cowdin, Mr J. M. Waterbury, Mr R. Agassiz, Mr L. Waterbury; and Rugby by Messrs C. and M. Nickalls, Mr G. A. Miller, and Mr P. Nickalls.

The English team, playing in great form, hit the first three goals in succession, and then the Americans had a turn, and in the third and fourth periods ... they secured the lead by hitting four goals in succession. Towards the end of the game Rugby had all the play, Mr G. A. Miller being in great form, and they eventually won by six goals to four.

In the other match Rugby, as above, met Roehampton – Mr Walter Jones, Mr A. Rawlinson, Mr Buckmaster, and Mr C. D. Miller. There was no score in the first period, nor did the play promise the fine struggle that was to follow. The feature of the game was the fine play of Mr A. Rawlinson and the steady defence of Mr Miller. Nothing better than these two players could be seen. It was a brilliant game, and the Prince and Princess of Wales stayed to the close.

This was the formal opening of the Club. The leading tournaments played at Roehampton are, besides the usual club handicaps, the Public Schools Cup, a series of matches which ought to grow in importance as the number of public-school men who play polo increases with each succeeding season; the Ladies' Nomination Tournament; and the Roehampton Cup, played for under the same conditions as the Rugby Cup. This tournament secures good entries, but in point of the number of teams competing, the Junior Championship is the most notable.

Indeed there are no more remarkable instances of the development of polo than the fact that the Ranelagh Novices' Cup and the Roehampton Junior Championship are the tournaments which secure the largest number of entries. Nor is this all, for both contests are noted for the very high average of play. In these matches you will see displayed combination, as well as individual skill and control of the ball. such as we should have looked for in vain a few years ago anywhere but in a first-class match, or in those members' games which were to be seen at Hurlingham in the years 1890–94.

The Roehampton Club started with everything to be done, but the managers report that they were able to improve the grounds during 1904, and that the practice ground has been levelled and boarded. The following, which is from the report of 1905, may give an idea both of the work done by the club and the development of the game in the last three years:

Polo began on 19th April, and continued till 28th July, during which time there were 83 playing days, and although polo was stopped on 15 days owing to wet weather, 104 matches were finished. The 1st Life Guards and 2nd Life Guards held their Regimental games on 18 different days, and 27 members' games took place. In all 167 different games and matches took place. The matches did not commence till May, so during the 12 weeks of the regular season an average was kept up of between 8 and 9 matches per week, and between 5 and 6 other games. During the whole season 6804 ponies entered the gates during the afternoons, and this does not include the very large number that used the club for practice in the mornings.

Besides the leading polo clubs with their luxurious surroundings, polo is played on several grounds near London, all of them somewhat less easily accessible than Hurlingham and Ranelagh, and having the common characteristic that they have no club-house or other accommodation for members than a pavilion more or less commodious. These clubs depend almost entirely on their polo grounds for attracting spectators. They have the advantage of making the game considerably less expensive, their subscription and entrance fees being, with the exception of Roehampton, not more than half those of the older clubs. Of these clubs the first to be established was Eden Park. The possession of an excellent polo ground, at one time the only one that was of full size, i.e. 300 x 200 yards, was a great advantage. Excellent management and the support of some keen and enthusiastic players gave this Club a success from its establishment.

For some time the Royal Horse Guards made Eden Park the practice ground of their team. There, were partly trained those admirable players who made up the four which held so strong a hand in the Inter-Regimental Tournaments of 1903 and 1904.

The Eden Park Club, which is near Beckenham, has one of the best natural polo grounds it is possible to conceive. The situation is picturesque, the turf is level, sound, and old, there are magnificent trees which shade the ground and give shelter to the waiting ponies. There are excellent stables for about seventy ponies and a most comfortable and well-arranged pavilion. The subscription is five guineas. The Club was founded by Mr Percy Bullivant and Mr L. Bucknall in 1897. The first manager was Colonel Sanders Darley, the present one is Mr F. Nash. Soon after the opening of the Club in 1897 one of those opportunities occurred that go far to give a club a start. As has been narrated elsewhere, the County Cup had passed into the hands of the County Polo Association. The Hurlingham Polo Committee, with but one match ground, did not at that time see their way to grant a day for a Cup no longer under their own control. It must be recollected that the Hurlingham Polo managers had already a heavy list of games and tournaments to provide for. Eden Park, several of whose members were on the council of the County Polo Association, opened its gates to the semi-finals and final of the County Cup, and before a crowded company one of the best matches in the annals of that Cup was fought out on the Eden Park ground. It was not merely a good county match but one of the best matches of the season, and one of the most exciting in the history of county polo. In offering their ground for the match, Eden

Park not only benefited themselves but gave a stimulus to county polo all over England. The Cup of 1898 drew an excellent entry. The earlier matches were interesting, for such teams as Rugby, Warwickshire, Chislehurst, Stansted, Feltham Park, Eden Park A were among the competitors. Of these Stansted, the holders of the Cup, and Chislehurst were left in the final. The afternoon of 14th July was a lovely one. The stand was full of ladies, and most of the best-known polo men were present. The turf was in excellent condition. There were some famous ponies playing, and the Stansted men were particularly well mounted. Mr Guy Gilbey made full use of his well-known No. 1 pony, 'Black Diamond.' Mr Tresham Gilbey, who never played a better game than he did that day as No. 3, rode 'Spinster,' one of the handiest ponies of the day, and a plain but very useful Argentine of the dun colour known as 'buckskin' in America.

Stansted had Messrs Guy Gilbey, P. Gold, Tresham Gilbey, and Gerald Gold; Chislehurst, Messrs Cecil Nickalls, H. Savill, M. Nickalls, and P. Nickalls. The latter team came from a new club and one that in the course of its brief existence has produced three first-class players in the Messrs. Nickalls. Stansted, having the greater experience, and perhaps better-trained ponies, were quicker on the ball than their opponents. Both teams were willing and able to gallop, and revelled in the freedom of the large ground. It was a fast game from start to finish. Stansted made a goal in the first few minutes and then came a desperate struggle. As Chislehurst gained confidence, so they improved their position. It was then that Mr P. Nickalls showed, for the first time, what a fine back player he is. With constant pressure on his goal he nevertheless kept the ball away from it. Yet it was a near thing. The ball was over the boundary line continually and several times Chislehurst hit out in self-defence. Then came the fateful third period. The young Oxford players – for I believe they all learned polo on Port

Meadow – had condition on their side. Chislehurst hit out, kept possession of the ball, and Stansted lost for a time their combination. It was Mr H. Savill, on a brown pony of the race of 'Hermit' that showed extraordinary smoothness of action and a great turn of speed, who hit the desired goal. It was again Mr Savill who saved the Chislehurst goal when the ball seemed to us, who were looking on, to be on the point of rolling over the line. After the fourth ten minutes Chislehurst gained the upper hand and won a close and exciting game.

Thus within a year of its start did Eden Park make itself a name in the history of polo, and its roll of members is now nearly six hundred. The Club has continued to prosper, and each year the manager puts forward an attractive list of matches. Such clubs as this have a great influence on the game, for they make polo known to many people who would otherwise never see it, and enable men to play the game at its best for a moderate expenditure.

The next club to be founded was the London Polo Club, at the Crystal Palace. The first managers were Major

The pavilion at Roehampton.

Polo ground at Roehampton.

F. Herbert, late 9th Lancers, and Major Cecil Peters, late 4th Hussars. Both were first-rate players, and Major Herbert had had considerable experience in the management of polo clubs. Both in Monmouthshire, which was one of the earliest of county clubs, and at the old and new Ranelagh Major F. Herbert had managed polo with success. The Crystal Palace ground is a good one, and except that it is more level is not unlike Hurlingham in shape. I have heard it argued by a most experienced player that an oval ground is really better for polo than the usual parallelogram. I do not, however, think that opinion can be sustained; nevertheless, we have seen some first-rate matches on the London Polo Club ground. The situation, too, has its advantages. A polo club should if possible not be isolated but have other clubs within reach, so that matches with visiting teams can be arranged. The London Polo Club has Woolwich and Eden Park within a reasonable distance, and ponies can easily be sent thither by road from Hurlingham and Ranelagh.

Then the London Polo Club keeps a good stud of ponies which can be hired by members. This is a great advantage to Indian and Colonial players who are making a short stay in this country, and wish to play polo in England without burdening themselves with a stud of ponies. Thus the London Polo Club has become international and cosmopolitan in its character. Some of the most noted Indian and Colonial players have been seen on its ground during the seasons polo has been played there, and several tournaments played at this club can compete with those at the older clubs both in the interest they excite and in the quality of play.

I pass on now to the English and Irish County Polo Associations, which will fitly conclude a chapter on polo clubs.

The County Polo Association is one of the chief notes of the advance of polo. In my chapter of recollections I have said that the establishment of this Association was one of the most important events in the story of modern polo. Nor do I think that this view is in any way an exaggeration. There were indeed a number of county clubs before the Association was formed, but many led a struggling existence. County polo needed support, regulation, and unity. Hurlingham was then to a certain extent in a state of transition between a private club and a public body, and the county clubs did not receive very much encouragement. For one thing, I do not think a great many people believed in the spread of polo beyond London and Dublin and a few favoured centres like Liverpool, Edinburgh, and Rugby. The idea was strongly fixed that polo was a game for men of money, and that it would never spread in the country on account of the expense. Two men, however, believed greatly in county polo, Mr Moray Brown and Mr Tresham Gilbey. I have often discussed the future of polo with them both. I think we saw that if polo depended on the favour of fashion, the tide which had borne it to prosperity might ebb as well as flow, and that the permanence of the game depended on its establishment in the country and on a wider basis. Much of the expense of polo was accidental, as I have several times pointed out. The necessary outlay on polo is not very large, and hardly out of the reach of any man who can afford to keep horses at all. The immediate occasion of the County Polo Association was the desirability of placing the County Cup on a firmer basis. The difficult point was to decide what should be the qualification of the players. On the one hand, it was necessary to exclude those players who, although they might be members of a club near to their country houses, yet were too strong for the average county team. It was evident that only a central body could make rules and regulations in the matter, and the County Polo Association was founded, with Mr Tresham Gilbey as its first president.

Very wisely the founders decided to have a committee room in London. They fixed on the West End headquarters of the P. and R. P. S. at No. 12 Hanover Square, and appointed Mr A. B. Charlton as Secretary. This step decided at once the success of the Society. It was plain that an Association whose affiliated clubs were as far apart as Edinburgh and Barnstable could have a common headquarters only in London. The stronger of the county clubs at once set the example by joining the Association, which gave to each club a voice in the election of the Committee of Management and thus a control over the affairs of the Association. How well the Committee have fulfilled their trust may be seen from the great success of the County Cup contest since it came under their control. The preliminary ties of the County Cup are played in the four divisions Northern, Midland, South-Eastern, and South-Western, into which the country is divided for the purposes of the tournament. The semifinals and final are played in London, and I have told how the final of the first County Cup under the new rules was played at Eden Park while Colonel Sanders Darley was manager. In 1899 the Cup was restored by the Committee to the Hurlingham programme, and the semi-finals and final have been played there ever since.

The affiliated clubs include all the leading county clubs, and the number steadily increases as new clubs are formed.

While the tournaments are arranged on the conditions laid down by the County Polo Association, the matches have always been played strictly under Hurlingham rules. The Hurlingham Club, when in 1903 it enlarged its Polo Committee, and gave to that body a somewhat more representative character, recognised the importance of the County Polo Association by inviting three representatives from among its members to join the Polo Committee. These representatives must be members of the Hurlingham Club. The County Polo Association not only accepted the offer, but has continually instructed its representatives to bring matters affecting the welfare of county polo before the central Polo Committee. Thus every member of an affiliated club has a means of being heard if he has anything of value to communicate. Several valuable suggestions have been made with regard to the measurement of ponies in this way, and by means of the County Polo Association Hurlingham is kept in touch with the various clubs scattered all over the country. Some of these are very large and powerful ones, and all include among their members many players who are never seen on a London ground. Rugby has 120 playing members, Leamington over 60, the Blackmore Vale more than 30, Liverpool 48, Cirencester 25, and there are many others. The probability is that the County Polo Association now represents a majority of the polo players of England. This will increase as polo gains fresh recruits in the country, and also as the younger men settle in life and giving up polo in London, still find pleasure in playing at their county club. The future of polo depends on the county clubs. They train the younger men and bring out the new ponies, thus causing a flow of fresh blood into the game. In the United Kingdom there are sixty clubs: sixteen are in Ireland, one in Scotland, and forty-three in England. Of these thirty-six may be considered to be county clubs, the others are soldiers' and sailors' clubs, or clubs like Hurlingham, Ranelagh,

Roehampton, Crystal Palace, which could not, of course, be reckoned among county clubs. Allowing an average of twenty playing members to each club (there are in reality perhaps rather more) this gives about 720 players as being represented by the County Polo Association in England and Scotland.

From English county polo I pass to polo in Ireland. The All Ireland Polo Club is the oldest existing club in the United Kingdom. It was founded in 1874. It was fortunate enough to secure a ground on that part of the Phoenix Park known as the Nine Acres, which has during the past year (1904) been greatly improved. This is, next to the match ground at Hurlingham, the most famous polo ground in the world. In one respect it even surpasses Hurlingham, for while both clubs have had almost every famous player and pony of the last thirty years playing there, the polo at Phoenix Park has been witnessed by many more people. The club ground has always been open to the public, and has ever been a great attraction to the sport-loving Irish people. The matches we have seen on the Nine Acres will never be forgotten. Moreover, this club has had more influence on the development of the game than any other except Hurlingham. Mr John Watson, who was the organiser of the game, was the leading member of the All Ireland Polo Club, and he had a chief voice in the original Hurlingham Club Rules. Thus Irish polo has never needed to draw up rules of its own, for the influence of its leading players has been and is still great in all legislation for the game. Indeed polo became almost from its introduction a national game in Ireland. They already had in Ireland a game called hurling, which is one of the games played on foot that is a direct descendant of polo. Indeed the early polo in Ireland was called hurling on horseback. There are points about hurling that mark its ancestry, and there is a use of the shoulder in hustling an adversary which will recall polo to any onlooker. When polo was introduced into Ireland it found congenial soil. The Irish players soon discovered that the game was as well adapted for Irish ponies as it certainly was attractive to Irish men. English players found that the Irish pony is the best for polo in the world. There was henceforth a market for a class of horses which had hitherto had few buyers. Now, Irish ponies are eagerly sought for and bought up for large prices. There are none to beat them when well trained, but they often have a touch of wilfulness and waywardness, just as young Irish hunters have.

In Ireland the county clubs have flourished and have enabled many people not only to play polo, but to make their fun pay its way by selling the ponies they have trained. What successful trainers the Irish polo players are, may be easily seen by going to Ireland and watching the County Cup ties or the Novices' Tournament, both of which cups are ruled by Irish County Polo Union rules, or by seeing the ponies that are brought over here every year by Mr John Watson and others. It is but seldom that one or other of the winners at the Hurlingham pony show is not an Irish-bred pony.

There are in all sixteen Polo Clubs in Ireland, of which twelve are affiliated to the Irish County Polo Union. These clubs represent about 300 players, exclusive of those regimental teams which are to be found playing in Ireland wherever garrisons are quartered. Thus Irish polo players are a very strong body of supporters of the game, both in quality and quantity. The matches of the County Cup in Ireland are the truest representatives of Irish polo to be seen.

Nor do the playing members represent the whole strength of the polo interest in English or Irish county polo by any means. Most polo clubs in the country have a large number of non-playing members. These are made up of players whose day is past, of lovers of sport, and of those people who find the County Polo Club a very pleasant meeting- place on a summer afternoon. Indeed, many clubs have established croquet grounds or tennis lawns, and all provide tea on open days. Then many clubs have an annual tournament, a pony show, a gymkhana, or a polo pony race meeting. These gatherings are greatly liked, and not seldom add considerably to the income of the club. On the whole, county polo, wherever it has been established, has distinctly brightened the dullness of life in country places.

But there is one thought that the multiplication of clubs brings home to us. We need some regulation of matches by the Central Committee. If at any time a spirit of rivalry or jealousy were to arise between the clubs, we might see on the one hand an undignified attempt to provide counter attractions on certain days, or an endeavour to prevent the best players from exhibiting their skill on the opposition grounds. It is only necessary to suggest the possibility of such a state of things, to make it plain how bad it would be for the interests of the game. The remedy lies in such an arrangement of the matches of the season as would prevent undue clashing and unseemly rivalry. We want in fact something of the same kind as is done by other governing bodies as to the arrangement and succession of cricket matches and race meetings. The present lists of matches are sufficiently large to suggest that there is a possibility of such a danger.

The London polo season has but three months. There are thus only twelve Saturdays available, even if they are all fine. Saturday afternoon is the time which makes or mars a club. People come down to lunch and to dinner, they bring their friends, and the gate-money is a considerable subsidy even to the revenues of a rich club. If we should have more clubs there must be competition for the Saturday crowd. But if these clubs all fix on the same Saturday for a Cup Tournament that means that many first-class players are in demand, and every polo manager knows how difficult it would be to divide out our leading players into the requisite six teams. Whereas, if the order of matches was controlled and to a certain extent mapped out before the beginning of the season by a central committee having weight and authority, each club would be able to arrange for first-class matches that should provide exciting and instructive contests for the spectators. We must not forget that polo is recruited and popularised by these first-class contests as much as by anything we can do for the game. If a man sees the pace, order, and skill of high-class polo he gains an idea of the game such as inferior players could never give him. Good matches are much more intelligible and instructive than inferior ones, and they set a high standard for ordinary players. The multiplication of tournaments in London and at county clubs has had the effect of raising the standard of play all round, and we now see better polo on many a county ground than any but the best players could have shown us in London a few years ago. The interests of all polo players alike seem to point to some authoritative and orderly arrangement of the season's fixtures, so that it might be possible to see at least all the best of the polo. But it is of course plain that the present Hurlingham Polo Committee could not do this, and we must wait for the day, not very far distant, when the progress of polo obliges us to have an All England Polo Association.

5
Regimental Polo

All that could be said or written on behalf of polo in the Army has been repeated so often that it need not be insisted on here. There are two points that if, and when, they are thoroughly understood are likely to cause the authorities and the public to look not unfavourably on the game as a recreation for soldiers. Of these two points the first is the training in horsemanship and horse mastership that the game provides when, as in accordance with the new rules laid down for army polo, regimental teams train their own ponies. The second is the economy of time and money. Polo is a game which occupies comparatively little time, and can be played in garrisons and camps. There is less temptation for an officer fond of polo and anxious for the success of his regimental team, to seek to be absent from his work, than any other recreation holds out.

The semi-finals and final of the inter-regimental tournament only demand a short leave from duty to be granted to four teams, i.e. sixteen men. Such matches as the Inter-Regimental, the Army Cup, and the Subalterns' Tournament take up but a few days at a time and occupy only the pick of army polo players. If we may judge the future by the past these men will also be among the best working officers, and thus precisely those to whom favours and indulgences would be most readily granted. When I claim for polo that it is not for soldiers an expensive game I shall not expect to escape uncriticised yet facts are on my side, and unsupported assertions and fancies are on the other. Polo is certainly less expensive than many other amusements, and the fact remains that officers who cannot afford to hunt can, and do play polo without spending more than they can spare on the game. The idea that polo is an expensive game has arisen from facts and incidents in the history of the game in England, which have nothing whatever to do with the actual expenditure of any individual player in His Majesty's service, or indeed outside it.

In the first place, polo is identified in the minds of most people with Hurlingham and Ranelagh. But these two clubs are much more than polo clubs; they are social clubs of a high class. They cater for wealthy people, and if the game could be played nowhere else it would by that fact be a game only for wealthy men. Nay, we may go further and acknowledge freely that it was in its early days confined to people of means. It was among that class that polo first took root, and it was a long time before the game spread sufficiently to enable men to take part in it with only a moderate expenditure of money. There were a few, very few, first-rate ponies bought at high prices. These animals were, with some exceptions, worth the money that was paid for them. But the price of the choicest animals does not set the standard for all the rest of their class. If no one hunted who could not give say 450 guineas apiece for his hunters, or no one drove a carriage who could not afford to pay 1000 guineas for a pair of horses, there would be only a few of us who would see hounds, and very many more who would go afoot than do so now. Even these famous ponies of which so much has been written were not expensive at first. 'Matchbox' was bought for £35, 'Little Fairy' cost about the same, 'Early Dawn' was once sold for £70, and how much or how little her original owner gave for her I should not like to guess, and 'Sailor,' of which I have written above, cost £30 in the first instance, and many more examples will occur to those who have had experience of polo.

The fact is that the raw material of a polo pony before he or she has been trained and polished is worth about as much as a good-looking ride-and-drive pony and no more. Naturally people tell us how much they sell ponies for, and preserve a judicious silence on what they paid. Again, all these high-priced ponies were, or were believed by good judges to be, extraordinary animals, and part at least of the price must be put down to the thorough training and sound judgment of those who bought and schooled them. The same is true of horses of all kinds, and a part of the price that is paid is given for the patience and skill of the rider or coachman who, having good material, has made the animals what they are.

This, then, is plain, that ponies in the rough need not cost more than a very moderate purse can afford. The training of them is a task, as I have elsewhere tried to show, not beyond the powers of a man with the gifts and tastes of a horseman. If at least one such man be not found in each of our cavalry regiments it would be a matter for surprise. I shall be reminded, however, that facts are in some respects against me, and a few instances may be brought forward in which a regimental team has purchased expensive ponies just before a tournament. In one instance at least this was done by a wealthy officer keen for his regimental team to win. But in any case I am not concerned to defend this, for the existing rules of the Army Polo Committee should prevent its recurrence. If the ponies are judiciously bought, and carefully trained, they will represent at any time the original outlay, and allowing for breakdowns and failures, a considerable percentage on the outlay.

But two other objections will be raised. You need, it may be said, so many ponies for polo that although each individual pony may not cost much, yet the price of five or six ponies for each man will mount up to a respectable sum. First, I will observe that the number of ponies required depends on two things – their quality and their condition. Well-trained ponies in hard condition will do a good deal of work at polo. We find in practice that in first-class matches players do really use very few ponies. Two ponies in practice matches and three or four at most in tournament games is enough. Of course in a regimental team the ponies would be supplied by the club, and the most suitable selected for tournaments. It would make for economy if all matches except the first-class ones were reduced from an hour to forty minutes, and if for Army polo the shorter Indian periods were adopted. Everyone knows how wearisome a long-drawn-out second-rate game at polo can be. Therefore nothing would be lost in interest by the change. I have seen a great deal of soldiers' polo in my time, and nothing can compete with it for interest. A good inter-regimental match will draw a better 'gate' to Hurlingham or Ranelagh than any other attraction. Something of the same kind may possibly stimulate play in a Hunt Cup or Public School Cup tournament, but the Oxford and Cambridge and the Public School matches have failed to catch on among university or public-school men at large. The inter-regimental tournament is, however, like no other, not only the players and their contemporaries, but almost every man who has served in one or other of the competing regiments and can attend, being certain to be there, as much interested as if he himself were still taking his turn with the belt.

The inter-regimental is a great occasion for the meeting of old friends and comrades, and is worth preserving if only for this. It is, moreover, notable that all who have had to do with ruling the army, whatever prepossessions and prejudices they may have had before they reach a position of authority, soon come to look favourably on polo. The game has been upheld by successive Commanders-in-Chief who have seen that, if sometimes it needed control, officers were willing loyally to observe necessary restraints. Indeed, many believe that both in England and India the game is the more prosperous for due control. For there are always some men who will go to extravagant lengths in any pursuit, and encourage weaker brethren to do the same. But for one man who has been led away from his duty by polo, there are hundreds who have succumbed to other attractions and temptations, which a diversion to polo might have counteracted.

Let us consider then what the actual career of a polo-playing officer is like when drawn from life, and not described by the vivid imagination of writers whose personal knowledge of polo or of the officers who play it is small.

The imaginary sketch of the last-joined trembling cornet ordered by severe senior subalterns to spend his last sixpence on polo ponies, or as an alternative to undergo much mental and physical torture, is absolutely unknown. The process by which a young soldier is taught to play polo is one that is familiar to every university man. It was, and no doubt is assumed still, that every man would be willing to do something for the honour of his college. He is asked in a friendly way to put his name down for instruction in rowing, and to attend at a certain hour at the college barge. The Captain of the Boat Club takes the freshmen out in turns in a tub pair, and expends a good deal of pains in teaching them to row. If the pupil is promising and willing, he is made to feel that everyone is anxious to help and to encourage him, and the prospect of a place in the Torpid or the Eight is held out as a goal for his ambition. This generally proves sufficient to keep the likely ones to their task, while the physically unfit, or those whose tastes lie in other directions, are weeded out. Not, however, as a rule before they have received some very useful training and discipline, and have engrafted in them a zeal for the success of their college on the river.

An exactly similar process goes on in most regiments. A subaltern, however lately joined, who is fit to be a soldier at all, is sure to be enthusiastic for the credit of the regiment, not only in the field but in games and sports. If polo is a tradition in the regiment, and the mess table has cups and trophies won by former teams, if stories are told of the great struggles of the past, the last-joined is fired by a zeal to do likewise. Of this spirit the seniors are glad enough to take advantage. The junior is mounted on a steady pony, fitted out with a polo stick, and set to practise under the eye of one of the best players in the regiment. With what kindly patience the youngster is encouraged, advised, and restrained, those who know most of soldiers' polo will best be able to tell. The chances are that, if he is anything of a horseman, or has a taste for riding, if he has had some practice at cricket, or better still at racquets, the best of all training for the working together of hand and eye, he becomes an apt pupil at polo. In all probability he will with difficulty be held back from buying, at extravagant prices, unsuitable ponies. His brother officers will help him to avoid the pit-falls which horse-buying brings in the path of the eager, generous, and unsuspecting subaltern, and he will be fitted out with one or two good ponies from the regimental club, the price of which is to be paid off by moderate instalments. Indeed, so far from the purchase of polo ponies leading to extravagance, instances have been not infrequent where men of moderate means have undergone considerable and salutary self-denial in the matter of wine and cigars, and even of short leave, in order to pay for the pony. Then as the chances of polo open out before him, it becomes clear to any sensible lad that polo is a game that demands condition in the pony and fitness in the man.

Thus he begins to look after the stable management of his ponies, and learns by practice to see that each horse requires special attention to bring him to his best. Some need more

The Lancers team.

food and less work, and others more exercise and less food. He learns to look after his pony's mouth and teeth, to see to the fit of the saddle, the suitability of the bit and bridle, to attend to the care of hoofs, and keep an eye on the blacksmith. He learns how to treat simple ailments such as over-reaches, bruises, etc., and is in fact in a fair way to become a horse-master. He learns too that success in polo depends on his own health and condition, and therefore begins to take rational care and exercise reasonable self-denial. So, too, he learns to keep his temper, hold his tongue, and obey the polo captain. Thus, insensibly, many of the qualities and acquirements of a cavalry soldier are infused into him while he is amusing himself. Always before his mind is the possibility of being chosen into his regimental team. Nor will his being a junior prevent that if he be fit for it. He will remember how J. Le Gallais and Maclaren and Capel Cure and many other notable names in polo records, found themselves playing for the regiment almost as soon as they had joined. If he is the son of rich parents he will learn self-restraint, and to help

others; if he comes of people of moderate means he will find
himself helped and encouraged in every possible way. The
best ponies in the regiment will be willingly placed at his
service, and if he is the owner of a good pony he may at least,
if not quite up to tournament form himself, obtain and enjoy
a vicarious satisfaction in the credit done to the regimental
team by the performances of his pony.

Nor is this any imaginary picture, for I know well a
good sportsman incapacitated by an accident from playing
in anything but cantering games, who draws the keenest
satisfaction out of the spectacle of a certain famous pony he
owns, playing in a first-class match with a first-rate player
to ride him and to do him justice.

Regimental polo is thus in peace-time one of the finest
disciplines to the individual, and one more bond between
an officer and his regiment.

I have seen in my time some very notable regimental teams:
the 13th Hussars, the 9th Lancers, the 10th Hussars, the
Queen's Bays, the Durham Light Infantry, the Inniskillings,
and the Royal Horse Guards. There are of course many
others, but these will suffice us as examples of regimental
polo, and I propose to sketch some reminiscences of the
famous matches I have watched these regiments take part in.

The last-named regiment has a great polo record, and
although they have never yet succeeded in winning the
Inter-Regimental, twice they have been very near. Their
polo team has produced some notable players. The late
Captain Rose, as good at polo as he was over the Quorn
country, with the same quiet style and resolute manner in
both sports, was an admirable No. 3, and his famous pony
'Yellowman' was one of the few first-rate snaffle-bridle
ponies I have known. Then there was the late Captain R.
Ward, a most brilliant horseman, whose runs on 'Black
Bella', or a bay blood-mare he had, made our blood tingle
with sympathetic ecstasy of pace. There were few No. 1

players to equal him in promise. The Duke of Roxburghe was an excellent player, who has, however, left the service, but not the game. Captain Marjoribanks is another fine player, whose 'Pilgrim' is one of the handiest weight-carrying ponies I have known, and he has often found favour with judges at the leading polo-pony shows. Major Drage, who played back in the Subalterns' Tournament when the regimental team won in 1897 and 1898, is a sound player. This player has also played for the Pytchley Hunt, with which the name of his family is connected. He used to be very fond of 'Sunshine', the grey mare that Lord Shrewsbury bought from Mr Buckmaster and sold to the Royal Horse Guards. The regiment has a most successful club, and a magnificent team of ponies, the property of the regimental club. They owe a great deal to the efforts of the late Major Ferguson and to Captain Fitzgerald (who often plays No. 3 for them) in organising and promoting polo in the regiment.

Their winning match for the Subalterns' Cup in 1897, and the gallant struggle the R. H. G. made with the 17th Lancers for the Inter-Regimental in 1903 and 1904, are matches that linger in one's mind. I think perhaps they were always at their best in public on the Ranelagh ground. They dearly love a galloping game, and with fast ponies, the space and liberty of that famous ground gave the team their best chance. But perhaps the finest soldiers' game I ever saw, which was said afterwards by one of the most experienced polo players among the senior officers of that day, to have been one of the closest struggles in his experience, was the final of the Dublin Inter-Regimental of 8th August 1895.

I shall not forget the occasion, for it was the first time I was entrusted with the task of describing an important polo tournament. Indian polo was familiar to me, and Hurlingham had been a daily duty during the season, but this was the first sight of an Irish polo ground.

I can therefore never forget the scene on the Nine Acres in Phoenix Park. It was my introduction to Irish polo, of which we had heard much in India. Such enthusiasm for polo I had never seen before. The crowd at the Inter-Regimental at Hurlingham was keen and interested, but it was apathetic in comparison with the popular gathering round the Dublin polo ground. Here were all sorts and conditions of Irishmen, all as keen and enthusiastic as possible, from the ragged urchins who sat at my feet to the occupants of the cars and carriages round the ring. Every player was known and each of them had his admirers. Captain (now Colonel) Malcolm Little of the 9th Lancers was a great popular favourite, and a more dashing forward never carried a polo stick. I well remember, as he dropped on to the ball near the rails and started for a run with a clear course to the goal, the delighted exclamation of a little capless ragged fellow who was crouched at my feet: 'Now, Little, by the Holy Fey, ye've got your welt!' The match of which I am writing was the final of the Irish Inter-Regimental, and was the more interesting that the two opponents, the 13th Hussars and 9th Lancers, had already met in the final of the All Ireland Polo Tournament.

The 13th Hussars had won the first match by a single goal. Now the same regiments were to try conclusions over again on the same ground. The teams were slightly altered, and they were arranged as follows:

9th Lancers	13th Hussars
Captain M. Little	Captain E. N. Pedder
Captain Claude Willoughby	Mr D. Robertson Aikman
Captain G. Colvin	Mr F. Wise.
Major Lamont (back)	Captain Maclaren (back)

Captain Little took the place at No. 1 of Mr (now Major) D. G. M. Campbell. It will be remembered that Major Campbell afterwards won the Grand National on 'The

Soarer' for another well-known polo player of those days, Mr W. H. Walker. The 9th Lancers played Major Lamont at back.

It is interesting on looking back to note the change that has come over the class of ponies that played then and now. There were several Arabs and barbs among the 9th Lancers' ponies, and, unless my memory deceives me, Captain (now Major) Maclaren was riding two country-bred ponies he brought from India. This was before the days of the 14.2 rule, but the ponies were if anything smaller than would be seen in a match of equal importance nowadays. I am not going to inflict on my readers the details of another match that was played many years ago, but I remember the keen excitement and the breathless tension with which the crowd followed a game every moment of which was full of pace and excitement. There were some wonderful strokes, for example, when Captain Maclaren, unable to escape from the forwards, hit the ball across the ground, darted after it and brought it back to the centre by a fine stroke across the pony's forelegs, then straightened it with a neat turn of the wrist and raced for the goal. The 9th were probably the stronger team, and possibly better mounted, but the combination of the 13th made them fully equal to their adversaries. The 9th Lancers won by a single goal made by Captain Willoughby, after the score had been marked as three goals all.

The season c.1893–c.1894 was a golden era in England for polo in the Army, and there was probably very little to choose between the 10th Hussars, 9th Lancers, and the 13th Hussars. The 10th Hussars have always been noted for their devotion to the game and their skill in it. The late Lords Airlie and William Bentinck, Lord George Scott, Colonel Kavanagh, and Major Brand were among the men I can recollect as the finest regimental players. They were in the first rank of polo players of the day. I can recall a notable feat of Lord George Scott's. He was riding a barb or Arab named 'Abdullah.' The pony was a plain-looking grey, but with far greater speed than he appeared to have. It is sometimes said that Arabs cannot hold their own with English ponies for pace, but 'Abdullah' was seldom beaten for speed. Lord George was racing on the ball with the goal not far ahead. (It was at Hurlingham, and the ground was somewhat cut up after several days of tremendous struggles in the Inter-Regimental Cup of 1894.) The ball began to bump, and twice Lord George Scott hit it with the cane of his mallet, sending it through the posts with the third stroke.

In 1888 I was at Sialkot, which was in that year a most interesting station from a polo player's point of view. We had two cavalry regiments stationed there, the Queen's Bays and the 14th Bengal Lancers, and there were two or three polo grounds. It was most interesting to watch the two teams, the Queen's Bays and the 14th Bengal Lancers, practically training each other in a number of friendly matches, and when in 1892 these teams won the Inter-Regimental and the Native Cavalry Cup respectively in the same year, there was great rejoicing in the station. The General of the Division was Sir Thomas Baker, who would have been Commander-in-chief in India had he lived, and the Brigadier the late Sir Power Palmer, who afterwards succeeded General Lockhart at Simla. Those who remember these distinguished officers will readily imagine that while the soldiering was of the best, sports were not discouraged, and polo least of all. The Queen's Bays had a brilliant team: Major Persse, now commanding the Egyptian Cavalry, was No. 1; Major Whitla, now 3rd Hussars, No. 2; Captain Bushe, No. 3; and Major Kirk, now 2nd in command of the regiment, was the back. All were fine players, and they took immense pains to mount themselves well. They practised steadily, were a very fast and brilliant team, and for a time quite invincible among British regiments.

One of the most interesting games at polo I saw the Bays play was in the final of the Punjab Tournament, the last time it was won by the 12th Bengal Cavalry. This was one of the very best polo teams that ever rode on to a ground. It was made up of three natives – all three, I think, non-commissioned officers in the Queen's service – and Captain Charles Gough. The three natives, Pretum Singh, Gurdit Singh, and Híra Singh, afterwards joined the Patiala team, becoming generals and colonels in the Maharajah's army. The late Maharajah of Patiala was an enthusiastic sportsman and loved pigsticking, polo, and billiards, and he mounted the three famous polo players on the best ponies money could buy. But I do not think the Patiala team at its best was ever equal to the 12th Bengal Cavalry four. Prosperity does not altogether agree with Sikhs, and the duffedars were certainly better players than the Colonels and Generals. I am not sure that I have ever seen a polo team in England or India that could have beaten the 12th Bengal Cavalry men at their best. They were admirable horsemen of the Asiatic type; they could hit the ball near side or off side with equal ease. Never have I seen anything like their control of the ball. Mr L. Waterbury, Mr W. Buckmaster, and Mr A. R. Rawlinson come nearer to this than any other players of our time, but I do not think any one of the three is the equal of Híra Singh. One peculiarity of this player was that you could not ride Híra off. He always either evaded you or hit the ball in spite of your best efforts. Major H. P. Sykes, a dashing heavy-weight who rode fast ponies, came the nearest to success. He swooped down on poor Híra and by weight of man and horse fairly pushed him off the ground.

But though the Bays could not win, they made a splendid game of it, and it was, I think, this match that inspired the Maharajah of Patiala with the idea of forming and training the team that was invincible for so long. The Patiala team were never defeated by English players until the 18th

Hussars succeeded in doing so. But I think that time, and perhaps good living, had somewhat impaired the condition of the Maharajah's famous four.

Of the teams I can recollect, none was more notable than that of the Durham Light Infantry. Patiala spent money without stint. The Queen's Bays, though never extravagant, bought some made ponies at fair prices. A well-managed and liberally supported regimental club enabled them to do so, and the judgment displayed was so sound that at their final sale the regimental polo club received about Rs. 18,000. Yet a cavalry regiment has advantages and opportunities for polo that no infantry can hope to enjoy. The Durham Light Infantry polo team were remarkable not only for their success, but also for the methods by which it was obtained, and for the comparatively small expenditure they incurred. It was generally recognised in India that Colonel De Lisle – now of the Royal Dragoons – was the directing mind and the moving spirit. It is clear that he found exercise and outlet, and I think it might be said training, for the abilities which he displayed as a leader in the Boer War, in forming the regimental polo team. The system was a stern one, the whole life of the regiment turned on the success of the polo team, other expenditure was discouraged, and even pig-sticking and steeple-chasing were regarded with disfavour lest they should disable by casualties men wanted to take a place in the polo team.

The training of the team was taken as seriously as that of a university crew. The men and ponies were kept in hard condition; early hours and careful living were enforced. Every man and every pony was fitted to his place in the team, and the combination of the four men was such as we have seen but seldom at polo. The 13th Hussars, the 12th Bengal Cavalry, and the Rugby team only among polo players have ever worked with such unity. But of them all in the matter of combination the Durham Light Infantry were the best. There was no passenger in the boat, and every man was always at work and with a single eye to team-play. They were the Ironsides among polo teams. Sometimes it was whispered that the rigidity of the rule irked some of them, but they obeyed, and the result was marvellous and such as no other team with equal or greater resources has ever achieved.

I do not deny that they were fine players individually, but this system made the best of them and made the best also of their ponies. It tried the ponies as well as the men, and I believe that about three or four seasons was the average time that a polo pony remained up to their standard. The ponies, like the men, had to obey and be easy to handle, and mere speed was not regarded as any substitute for the power to turn, willingness to stop, readiness to start, that mean so much at polo. It is not likely that we shall soon again see a team which combines such perfection with fitness of condition. Yet the main principles of the Durham Light Infantry training must always be those which lead to success. One thing, however, readers must bear in mind, – that their victories were won under the Indian system of brief periods (five minutes) and short matches (forty minutes), which permits a closer concentration and a severer strain than our longer periods.

There are, of course, many other notable teams and incidents in the story of Army polo. There are, for example, the 7th Hussars, who have been on the whole the most successful in winning tournaments. This regiment supplied three out of the four players who went to America for the first international match. They have won the Inter-Regimental Cup both in England and India – the former five times, the latter twice. They are the only regiment that ever won three cups in their first season in England or India. They have produced many notable players, including Major Poore, who would be a great polo player if he were not so distinguished a cricketer and so keen a soldier. His great feat of hitting the winning stroke in the final tie of the Inter-Regimental Cup for the 7th Hussars at Hurlingham, and making a hundred runs for Hampshire at County Cricket during the same week in 1899, is not likely soon to be either surpassed or forgotten.

I do not propose here to go over again the old but never to be forgotten story of the way in which polo players won distinction in the Boer War. But there can be no doubt that the unquestioned facts have made a due impression on those who have to rule the Army. The Army Polo Committee has been formed in order that polo may be restrained, controlled, and encouraged. Sir Edward Ward, the Secretary of the new Army Committee, joined the Committee of the Ranelagh Club in 1904. At the same time no doubt there will be a real control of expenditure in this as in other matters. While the Army Polo Committee serves as a link between the authorities and the great body of soldier players, the regimental polo pony clubs seem to offer an opportunity for control of the share taken by individual members. The usual system of a regimental club at present is as follows: Every member pays 10s a month as subscription, and if he desires a pony, £10 a year as hire. The club borrows a sum of £1000, and the interest and instalments are paid off out of the income arising from the hire of the ponies and the subscriptions of the members. In practice this has been found to work well. For example, regiment borrowed £900. In the course of a few years they found themselves clear of debt, with an income of £250 wherewith to purchase remounts. After several successful polo seasons the regiment was transferred to India. The sale of the ponies realised £1200, leaving thus an ample sum in hand to purchase ponies in India.

It seems to me that it would be wise to give these clubs official recognition and some control. The accounts might be open to the Inspector-General of Cavalry, and the Colonel would be responsible that the subscription was voluntary. The management of the club, the inspection of the ponies, and the buying of new ones are entrusted to a committee, and this work is no bad training for a cavalry soldier. No regiment that had not a recognised and approved club in full and satisfactory working order should be permitted to send a team to the Aldershot Cup, the Inter-Regimental, or the 'Subalterns' Tournament. A further step might well be taken. The Government might lend a certain number of 14.2 ponies to the poorer clubs, receiving the £10 for hire, and retaining certain rights over them. A good polo pony, well trained, is already nearly a perfect mounted infantry cob. Thus a large reserve of high-class cobs would be in readiness for war time. Without expense a couple of thousand ponies might easily be distributed if the yeomanry were included in the grant. The ponies would have to be selected by someone who knew what a polo pony was and ought to be. If, as I have sometimes heard it said by experts, in the next war we shall need at least 10,000 ponies for mounted infantry, then it is evident there ought to be a reserve somewhere. Polo offers the opportunity, the ponies would be kept for nothing, and the money paid for their hire would probably cover the outlay of their purchase. In addition a very much better class of pony would be obtained than most of those now in the army. A really good polo pony is easy to ride, and that is no small consideration in the case of men who are not (as mounted infantry cannot be) professional horse soldiers.

There is no such cob in the world as our English riding ponies, and no such schooling as polo gives them. The risk would be very small, for very few polo ponies break down, and the majority last in full vigour for many years. The casualties among polo ponies are far less than among any other class of horse with which I am acquainted, and to this I think all who have had experience will agree.

But to return for a moment to the regimental polo clubs. They are practically co-operative societies for the benefit of officers. The question still remains as to who is the right person to buy the ponies. This may be done in two ways. The first and most obvious is to appoint one man of polo experience and proved judgment to buy all the ponies. But there is this objection to such a plan, which was put forward by General Rimington in an excellent article on the subject contributed to *Baily's Magazine* in March 1897, 'It does away with individual effort.' Such a plan would work fairly well if the regimental ponies were to be all trained ones. But they are not, and if good ponies are to be bought for moderate prices the ponies must be untrained. Officers should be encouraged to look out for ponies likely to make polo ponies. Incidentally they will learn a great deal in doing so about the sources and extent of our horse supply. Each officer should be instructed to find out all the available ponies round his own home. A maximum price should be fixed and paid by the club. The training of the pony should be entrusted to the man who bought it. If, when trained, it was passed into the club by the Committee, the officer would have nothing to pay beyond his subscription to the club. If, on the other hand, the pony was rejected, it would be sold, and the purchaser would be liable for the difference between the selling price and what he had given for it. This would probably not be great in any case. Naturally, such a rule would make men careful, and there would be considerable emulation as to who should buy the best pony. If an officer bought for himself he would still be obliged to have the pony passed by the club before it was allowed to play in the regimental game.

By some such plan as this the utmost benefit would be obtained from regimental polo, and we might hope to see it stand as high as it ought to do in the favour of all sensible men.

6

The Training of the Pony

The subject of this chapter is one of increasing importance. Every year well-schooled ponies become more necessary to modern polo. Speed is much, but handiness is more. It may be questioned whether a team on well-schooled ponies would not in the long run beat one mounted on more speedy but less easily controllable animals. But handiness is not entirely a matter of well-schooled ponies; it depends, more perhaps than is usually admitted, on the horsemanship of the rider. Now the best school of practical horsemanship is the breaking of young horses.

It was not only motives of economy which made the Army Polo Committee lay down the rule that regiments were, as far as possible, to train their own ponies, but because the lessons of horsemanship and horse-mastership taught by polo are only to be learned by the man who trains and makes his own ponies from first to last. The great argument for polo in the army is its value in this respect, and if men are to buy ready-made ponies the ground is cut away from under the feet of its defenders.

Nor is there anything new in this. The men who made polo what it is schooled their own ponies, for in the early days of polo there was no other way of gathering a stableful of ponies than by purchasing them in the rough and training them to the game yourself. It was in this way that most of the early players obtained the famous ponies of which we have heard. It has already been related that the Messrs

Lady Jane's Toilet.

Lady Grey, a good 'back' pony.

Peat bought and trained their famous stable of ponies. Lord Harrington, Mr T. Kennedy, and Mr Kenyon Stow gave much time and thought to schooling the ponies by the aid of which they helped to win so many matches. Regimental teams in India trained their own ponies, which were bought in the rough at Indian fairs and from dealers at Lahore or Bombay. In India the majority of players trained their own ponies, and probably do so still.

The present chapter, then, is intended to suggest that what has been done by others can be done by ourselves. Indeed, if a man of moderate means is to play polo at all he must school his own ponies. It has already been laid down authoritatively that, if polo is to continue to flourish in the Army, and to grow under the sunshine of official smiles, then officers must learn to make ponies into polo form.

But, be that as it may, there is no doubt that the majority of would-be players will be likely to read this chapter with some interest. It is quite possible that this work may fall into the hands of some man who has seen polo and felt its charm. No one who loves riding can look on at a really fine match without desiring to join in the game. The pace, the keen struggle for the ball, nay, the eager rapt expression on the faces of the players, speak for polo to many a man who has given up such games as cricket and football. The one difficulty is to buy the ponies. I do not mean that there is much difficulty in finding a pony, but when we have him he is not a polo pony. The prices of the leading dealers are out of our reach. We cannot afford to fit ourselves out at Rugby, with three ponies at a cost of anything from £500 to £1000 for the three. No doubt we shall obtain what we pay for. But we can hardly expect to have the skill and judgment and time of the Messrs Miller, or Withers, or Rich, for nothing. Nor do I say that it is not worth paying for. On the contrary, if a man has money and not too much time, he cannot do better than buy from those who know what a polo pony ought to be. Yet I think perhaps there is more pleasure and satisfaction in finding and making our own ponies than in obtaining them ready made. If we are successful none will ever suit us as well.

I have seen it written and heard it said that it is a very difficult thing to make a pony into a good polo pony. There is a difficulty, which is to find the raw material. Horseflesh of high quality is never very easy to buy, but it can be found, as everyone knows who has tried. We have most of us had good hacks and hunters and harness horses, and there are still good ponies to be found. They are all round us if we have eyes to see. Not polo ponies yet, but animals that can be made into polo ponies. Some men, however, may be discouraged by the obstacles. 'We are,' they will say, 'fair judges of a horse, but we are not first-rate polo players, or anything like it, and therefore even if we have the pony we cannot do anything with him.' There is no greater mistake. It is not necessary to be a player of skill in order to make a polo pony. Certain things are necessary, but it is not needful to be able to play in first-class company. Some excellent pony trainers that I have known were very indifferent performers in the game. What is required is fair horsemanship, great patience, much perseverance, and a most careful attention to details. Most ponies that have anything like true make and shape will make polo ponies if they are treated in the right way.

When buying a pony we must note certain defects that cannot be passed over. It is true that some oddshaped ponies have turned out well, but the chances are against this, and our would-be polo player does not profess to have such skill at the game, such mastery over the ball, that he can rectify the failings of his mount. I am sure from the ponies I see exercising in the roads in the spring, that there are a great many men wasting their time and trouble over animals that will never really do them credit. At the same time, you must

take the descriptions you read in books with a grain of salt.
The animals there painted in glowing words are not likely
to come your way. To quote from the experience of a player
who is playing regularly in first-class polo,

> 'by buying ponies which I think are really right for polo,
> I have never had a single failure. All have played well
> in first-class polo, though, naturally, all have not been
> perfect in shape, and consequently all have not been
> equally valuable. Some have not withstood the strain so
> well as others; some are up to less weight; but all have
> played well in first-class polo, which is a very high test
> when we consider that they were often pitted against
> ponies costing £500.'

The first thing to consider about a pony that is offered
is, supposing this was a horse would I buy him to hunt
on? Does he look like galloping? Weedy, ill-coupled ponies
should be avoided, so should ponies with short thick necks,
or those that carry their chins against their chests. Short
straight pasterns are serious defects; long sloping pasterns,
on the other hand, even if they look a little too long and a
trifle weak need not put us off. A polo pony is better short
in the back, but I have known some ponies that looked a
little long do very well, and you cannot have everything. A
good-tempered, sensible head, properly carried, and a well-
placed neck would at any time go a long way with me. Since
perfection is not to be obtained, one point must balance
another. Nor is it advisable to be entirely guided by the eye.

If you are not quite pleased with the pony's shoulders never
mind, but jump on to its back and see how it uses them when
trotting down a rough slope with a loose rein, and note how
it places its feet, and whether it goes boldly without tripping
or stumbling. There is, of course, no perfection that you
would not desire; there are also few you cannot do without.

If a pony walks well and trots easily you may take a good deal on trust, and you may be pretty sure that you will have to forgive something, or at least to try to forget it.

It may well be that in buying ponies in the rough you may not be able to have much of a trial. If you want to pick up ponies cheap you must be prepared to buy them when you see them, and as you can. The less trial you are able to have the better looking ought the pony to be. It is, of course, quite true that we have all owned ponies and horses that we should never have purchased unless we had been on their backs. They win us by their action, their lightness in hand, the spring of their movement, and we know then, if no obvious or fatal defect is visible, that the eye is deceived. Yet I should never buy a pony for polo that did not carry its saddle fairly well, or that had, as I have said above, a thick short neck. Last of all, I should never buy one that showed temper or sulkiness. It matters very little to you whether these faults are natural or acquired by bad usage. Eagerness and impetuosity may also be incurable faults, but that you cannot always tell beforehand. They are developed by the excitement of play. Wonderful transformations I have known in excitable animals by gentle and judicious handling and a polo pony should be willing and eager. Lazy ponies do not, as a rule, make good polo ponies.

It is well, however, to study the type we require. There is no better object lesson than to go to one of the leading clubs when members' games are being played. Round the pavilion there will be grouped about a hundred ponies, each of which is more or less of a true type. In order to buy such ponies you must keep your eyes open and take them when you can find them, with or without a trial. You must go about and look for them. The hunting field, country towns on market days, horse repositories, Galloway race-meetings, are all possible places. You never know when you will or will not find a treasure. The wise buyer, if he has a little grass round his house, will not refuse a promising youngster if the price is right. Mares and fillies are better than geldings. If there is accommodation for them at home it is no bad plan to buy a promising three-year-old filly, sending her to a good polo pony sire, if you have one in your neighbourhood. She will not be ready for polo till five, and you may have a nice youngster to the good. Those ponies that you believe or know to have a strong infusion of pony blood, nearly always make the best polo ponies. It used to be the fashion to pooh-pooh pony blood, but now all those who have studied the subject know that some pony blood runs in the veins of most of our best polo ponies. This at all events is certain, that if you are bent, as I think wisely, on making your own ponies, those with some Welsh or Exmoor, Dartmoor, or New Forest blood in their veins, will certainly come to your hand more easily and readily than the thoroughbred dwarfs and misfits which four or five years ago were the common ideal of what a polo pony ought to be.

Once having obtained the pony, the next step is to train it. Let us ask ourselves what a polo pony ought to be able to do. To hear some people talk, one might be tempted to imagine that to train a polo pony was a feat as difficult as to play the violin. In truth it is quite simple and well within the power of any man who has patience, perseverance, and horsemanship sufficient. The training for polo is merely the thorough breaking and education that every horse should have. The greater part of the process is in no way different from careful and systematic schooling, such as most horses would be the better for. The pony must learn to go in a collected form in all his paces, to become, in fact, as perfect a hack as possible. A polo pony has other special duties. A horse, however, can only learn one thing at a time and very little of that. A general education should go before special accomplishments.

The first thing to do is to make friends with him and to

make him gentle and familiar. A horse is by nature nervous, he is not fearful until he has been made so by ill-usage. There is no necessity to disturb ourselves as to whether a horse is capable of attachment to his master. I believe he is, but many authorities think he is unable to rise above the kind of affection known in the nursery as cupboard love. To search into motives is needless. The point is that we should be able to handle the pony without any apprehension arising in his mind that we mean to hurt him. The man who has to handle and break many horses will find that he can do much by quiet restrained movements and gentle speech. Always speak to a horse before you go into his box, and talk to him while you handle him. If the pony is entirely unbroken his first lessons should be with the lunging rein. I know that this has fallen rather into discredit, but there is nothing better to give the first lessons with than the lunging rein. It is of course; best to begin in a school for breaking horses in. Their attention is not distracted; there is nothing to startle them. The common mistake made in lunging is that horses are kept too long at their early lessons. Ten minutes or a quarter of an hour is ample. In fact, as soon as the pony will trot round, first in one direction and then in the other, quietly and steadily, the lesson should be brought to an end. Even if the pony has nominally been broken to saddle or harness I should still lunge him for a quarter of an hour twice a day for a week. This teaches him to do his work steadily and to obey, which is the foundation on which all our teaching must rest.

In these early lessons you will have kept steadily before you that in training a pony for polo the point to which particular attention should be paid is the training of the pony's disposition. If, by injudicious treatment, you spoil in any degree your pony's temper, he is by so much the less suitable for polo. The very fact that a horse's intelligence is limited and his memory retentive should make us more careful of his training. Just as we have to be more careful of

Matchbox. This pony played in seven open cups. Bred in Yorkshire pedigree unknown.

our speech to a dull or stupid man than to a clever one, so it is easier to spoil a horse in his training than the more intelligent dog. The union of courage, limited intelligence, and a highly strung nervous organisation which marks the horse among domestic animals should be the guide to our treatment of him. We must not forget that the intelligence of animals, though (perhaps because) it is limited, is within those limits more effective than ours. An animal when undisturbed by fear or fatigue desires always to do what it can as well as it is able. Moreover, as the constitution, so the temperament of every horse varies, and each is different from the other.

As I am not writing for dealers and those who have to do with horses in considerable numbers, but for men who wish to train a few ponies, not more than one or two at a time, for their own riding, it is quite easy to study the idiosyncrasies and peculiarities of each subject. In this way, taking the methods noted above in relation to each pony, we shall be able to modify and adapt them. Inasmuch as the case supposed here is that of a man who has no ulterior object in view beyond making as good a polo pony for his own use as possible, the method is much simplified. When we come to ride the pony the first thing to do is to see to the bitting and saddling. I am a great believer in the use of a roomy, comfortable saddle that fits the rider. I have had many saddles, some new and some second-hand, but the fault I generally find is that the saddles are too short. A comfortable saddle for the man is a great point in the education of the pony. The more easily the rider is able to sit the less will he be likely to worry the pony's mouth. I have put the comfort of the rider first because I have never found any difficulty in having a well-made hunting-saddle stuffed to fit a pony by the nearest saddler. Each pony you train should have his own saddle, and as his condition improves the stuffing should be carefully looked to, as pain or inconvenience upsets a horse's temper and distracts his attention, and our aim must be to have an animal thoroughly tractable to our will. There are moments when compulsion must be used as in the hunting-field, but so far as is consistent with always being master, it should be used as little as possible with the polo pony. It is at this point that privately trained ponies have the advantage over those which are educated with a view to selling. They can have more individual attention expended on them.

From the saddle we pass to the bit. There are many fancy bits in the market, but for the privately trained pony there is only one – the ordinary double bridle we use in the hunting-field. The cheeks may be longer or shorter according as the pony is more or less eager by nature, for we must always be able to stop a polo pony. The best of all are those keen, high-couraged ones that want to gallop, but these are exactly the ponies that need the most control. Yet a dead pull on the reins should always be avoided as far as possible, and therefore the bit must be sufficiently powerful to make the pony throw his head up at once when checked. This should be done with a sharp, but not violent jerk, never with a steady pull, because all we have to do is to convey one's wishes to the pony without deadening his mouth. It is well always to speak sharply when we check the pony, and after a time we shall find that raising the hand and speaking will steady him without any pull on the mouth at all. One of the first things a polo pony has to learn, and perhaps it is necessary for the rider as well, is that his work must be done with a loose rein. The pony should never begin to learn how to pull. It is evident that all this can be taught quietly when riding along the road. The fact is, in the earlier stages of the training all we have to do is to ride the pony whenever we can. As we trot or walk along the road we should be always feeling the pony's mouth, and endeavouring with a gentle pressure of the legs to force him up to his bit, and to bring his hind legs under him, so that in all paces which we are likely to use – trot, walk, and canter – the pony shall be going with a light forehand. This we can do simply by bearing in mind, when riding over the farm or going to covert, that the pony will someday be wanted for polo. The best understanding will spring up between us and our ponies, since we shall never be the cause of needless pain or suffering to them. The rides will be equally a pleasure to both, and while we are hacking about day by day the pony will be growing into condition and putting on muscle. I strongly deprecate anything but general training when a pony is weak or out of condition.

When the time comes to give the special training needed for polo the pony ought to be fit and full of life, while he will scarcely know if there be another will than that of his rider. If during the preliminary period the pony shows signs of an obstinate and sulky temper; if, without any fault of yours, he puts his chin in his chest and pulls against you; if you discover any faults of action, then I should say his education was not worth proceeding with, and I should break him to harness and sell him. The chances are that his vocation in life is that of an ordinary ride-and-drive pony.

When you can do anything with him on the road, then comes the next step, the special education needed for a polo pony. You are now on the best of terms with your pony. By this time you ought to know for certain whether he is likely to suit you for the game. I found in practice that, after a little time, I could generally tell whether a pony was worth persevering with or not. The probability is that he will be. The failures are the minority. A pony that would perhaps be rejected by an experienced dealer in polo ponies as not worth his trouble might, in a private stable, turn out very well.

In the case of the dealers time is money, and most of them prefer buying ponies more or less readymade. They know where to place them at a profit. But the object of this chapter is to help a man to make a pony for his own riding.

The best time to begin a pony's education is in the autumn. You have then a whole winter before you, in which to give the pony a variety of work. Nothing is better than a trot or canter to covert, though you must not start late and gallop eight or ten miles. What can be better than a ride to covert? He comes out of the stable head up, ears pricked, with that look of alertness so characteristic of a pony. After a little preliminary play you find a soft side to the road and trot along. The action is smooth and springy, the head carried well up. Answering to a light check with the hand and pressure of the legs the pony brings his hocks well under him, you see his shoulders working freely, and he steps over the ruts as though treading on air. Then we turn off from the road and a gate has to be opened, and gate opening is an excellent exercise for man and beast. Then comes a stretch of soft turf, and a fast canter may be indulged in. Yet we are still careful as to the form the pony goes in, and do not go too fast.

I believe it to be one of the cardinal maxims of polo-pony training that a pony should not gallop his best except in the game. This does not apply equally to ponies that have learned their work: I have known several ponies that could be taken from racing to polo, and would play as steadily and well as could be desired. But the treatment of the older pony naturally permits of more liberty than that of the younger.

But to return to the road to covert. You should be having a delightful ride, noting the advance your pony has made in training, or perceiving faults that need attention. It is quite probable that with a young pony, and particularly if it comes from Ireland, there may be a little exhibition, we will not say of temper, but of waywardness. After looking about him the pony sees, or pretends to see, something very startling, stops, wheels round, and tries to make off home. As the rider who has to think of the education of his mount is probably on the alert, he meets the attack by bringing his hunting crop down on the pony's shoulder and, speaking sharply, tightens the reins. If this is done quickly enough it probably checks the incipient rebellion, and there is no further trouble. But if a pony has succeeded to ever so slight a degree in an act of rebellion he will try it again, and it will save trouble if we are beforehand with him. Thus the hesitation and the gathering of himself together before the turn round may be stopped at once by a word, a check on the bridle, or a slight touch with the spurs. But if the pony has come round, then two or three strokes down the shoulder accompanied by a sharp word will be necessary. This is not a case for patience but for instant action.

The best polo ponies are often mares. I had almost written always, but I recollected 'Cyclops,' 'Piper,' 'Sailor,' and 'Johnnie' in time. Nevertheless, of the ponies playing at any one time, of those that hold a high place in the estimation of polo players, the probability is that the majority are mares.

We ought to be very much more patient with mares than geldings. They are, as one might expect, much more wayward than the latter, but their tricks mean less. They are extraordinarily sensitive to the voice – a word is often enough where a blow would be needed with the other. I am always very unwilling to hit a mare, and have more than once succeeded in training one without using the ash plant at all. In any case, I believe it is a sound rule never to hit a horse more than twice or thrice at one time.

If the rider can be sure, which is not always the case, of not using them unconsciously, I should advise the use of sharp spurs during training. Spurs are good on the principle that prevention is better than cure, for a sharp touch of the spur will often nip a possible rebellion, and cause a horse to spring forward in a way that gives an opportunity to the rider. Spurs have fallen into disfavour, yet I think they should always be worn on the road. The disuse of spurs I attribute to two causes. First, because the long straight spurs which 'are the fashion are really dangerous. They are very smart, and as dummies useful, but when I wish to use sharp spurs I prefer the old-fashioned short spur slightly bent downward. The other reason is that spurs are thought to be cruel, and this, not because they hurt the horse more than a whip or stick would do, but that they pain the spectator more. Yet the drop of blood on a thin-skinned horse is probably the evidence of far less suffering to the animal than the weals inflicted by an ash plant or a cutting whip. Of course there are men who are neither to be trusted with whip nor spur, but if I had doubts about a man's temper, and had to put him on a horse that required stimulating, I would rather put spurs on his heels than a whip in his hand.

By this time the pony, hacked about and exercised, should be in fair condition, accustomed to various sights and sounds, and it has possibly even been hunted with harriers. I do not think, however, that it is a good plan to hunt quite young ponies while in training for polo. It is one of the conditions of success that the pony shall be fresh on its legs, that these should be neither shaken nor sore. An old pony may be hunted without any fear of doing harm when the ground is soft. Yet I am strongly in favour of a winter's rest for old ponies, if the pony can be spared. But we have to balance advantages, and if the pony is wanted he must be worked. I prefer harness work for old ponies, provided the cart be so balanced as to throw little or no weight on the back. For most ponies steady road work, say in a four-wheeled dog-cart, or as leaders in a team or tandem, is useful exercise. But it must be remembered that we are now dealing with ponies, possibly young ones, and that everything we do is directed to one object, to make polo ponies of them. Incidentally, we shall be in possession of a pony so well schooled that it can be adapted for any purpose for which it is required.

When once the trainer is satisfied that the pony has learned all he can teach him in the school or on the road, the first part of the training is over. Before beginning the second part it is no bad plan to let the pony have a rest of a fortnight or so, and if the ground is fairly soft a meadow or paddock is not a bad place to take it in. Then, when he comes up again, go quickly over the lessons of the past two or three months to see that the pony is tractable, and to prevent his coming to the second stage of his education when above himself.

The general training is now over, and after we have had some experience we shall be able to judge whether we can make anything of the pony for polo purposes. If we think it unlikely that the pony will make a really useful polo pony it is better to let him go to other work. Our object in training a pony is to enable us to enjoy the game, and it is a mistake to be drawn aside by anything from this purpose. In the end it is far more economical to sell an unsatisfactory pony and to try another, than to persevere when our common-sense and knowledge of horse-flesh tell us that only a limited success, if any, is possible. But if we are satisfied that the pony will suit us after all, then it is time to take the next step forward in his education. This is to accustom him to the stick, and about this there should be no trouble. If, as suggested above, the pony has been trained with spurs, and has not been accustomed to regard the right hand uplifted with a stick as a preliminary to punishment, there will be very little difficulty. I have never known a case of a pony that refused to allow you to use a polo stick, unless he had been hit about the legs and head with it. In this case it is not wonderful if he has a dislike to the stick. Of course, everyone has known ponies that were stick shy, but, to speak from my own experience, I have found that even in the case of Indian country-breeds – surely the most nervous of horses – there was but little difficulty in accustoming the ponies to allow a stick to be used from their backs. The rules of polo lay down the regulation that players are not to strike their ponies with the head of their sticks. The man who trains ponies will be well advised if he abstains from the use of the cane as well. A pony forgets nothing, and, to say the least, being hit with any part of the stick is not likely to make him fond of the game. An old hardened pony with his habits well set, and that may, for all we know, be as fond of the game as his master, and will stand a good deal. Habit goes for so much with horses, but the young, fresh pony is nervous and, because everything is strange, easily scared.

To return to the stick. Mounting the pony in the field or paddock we have set apart for training our ponies in, and carrying a polo stick in the right hand, we ride at a trot and canter until the pony is prepared to go steadily. There is likely to be a little effervescence of spirit at the first start off. If so all the better, but that is not the time to begin swinging a polo stick. As soon then as he has steadied down swing the stick about, first below the level of the saddle as though hitting a ball along the ground. Why not have a ball as well and thus save time? Because all the rider's attention must be fixed on so managing the stick that it shall not hit the pony, and if there is a ball in rough ground it is difficult to avoid doing this sometimes. One thing at a time is an excellent rule for polo-pony training. In the next place, we should from this time forth carry a polo stick whenever we ride, or any long walking stick with a fairly heavy handle will do as well.

Then we have to consider what the next steps ought to be. Three things are chiefly required of a polo pony – that he should start quickly, turn sharply, and that he should gallop smoothly and steadily on the ball. Leaving the last for the present we have to consider the second of the three. The pony must turn sharply on the signal given. The first thing is to teach him to change his legs. To begin with, he should be walked, trotted and cantered slowly in a wide figure of eight. Choose a space of turf as smooth as possible, and place two polo balls at about twenty yards apart. Take the reins in both hands at first. Make a complete circle round, one say from right to left, then a circle from left to right round the other. Go on at this, using circles of about the same size and riding at the same even pace until the pony describes the circles easily and smoothly, changing his leg as the pressure of the right or left leg of the rider indicates, and without any more pressure of the bit on his mouth than the lightest. A touch of the reins and the signal given by the rider's leg are the signs he is wanted to obey. This is simply a matter of practice for the pony. He requires to learn to do it by frequent repetition. When he will do this readily and easily, starting either way and acting in complete obedience to the signals given by the rider, the pace may be increased, but it is not necessary or even desirable to try for great speed. When the action of changing his legs is so habitual as to become as it were instinctive, so that the response to the rider's will is ready and instantaneous, and he will make the change with but the slightest, if any pressure on the bit, the lesson is learned. But a day of his instruction should never pass without a figure of eight at a steady pace. If the lesson is thoroughly learned he will change his leg as quickly and as surely in the game, when galloping at high pressure, as he does on the practice ground. There should in time be neither perceptible effort nor resistance in his action when turning. The circles should be reduced in size so as to make the turns quicker, but they need not be made too small. There should always be room for the pony to stride round comfortably.

I have said that in carrying out this exercise the pony should have as little pressure on the reins as possible, but this must be qualified by the consideration that with big and awkward ponies we have to be careful that they go in collected form, with their hocks well brought under them and a light fore-hand.

If pains have been taken with the preliminary training of the pony then it ought to be in the habit of moving in true form. These figures of eight having been thoroughly mastered, the pony ought to be prepared for at least the ordinary occasions of the game.

But there are frequent occasions for sharper turns than a pony will make when cantering in a circle, and for these I propose a further exercise. Plant four posts in the ground so as to mark the corners of a parallelogram. Suppose then that A, B, C, D are the four posts. Start from A, springing off into a sharp canter, ride to B, check the pony, and bringing him sharply round ride back diagonally to D, then from D to C and C to A, trying not to go beyond the post and to come round and be off as quickly as possible. The pony should be checked at B and D. It is evident that this will admit of a variety of exercises giving practice in starting, stopping, and turning, thus – this exercise is an admirable one, for it rehearses a situation not uncommon at polo. As a rule, I prefer that the distance should be considerable, say, fifty or sixty yards from A to B, and C to D, or even more. That the practice at this should not be prolonged at one time, and that the distances should be frequently varied, are suggestions which everyone will see the force of.

By the time that a pony can do these exercises easily, willingly, and without hesitation at the turns, he will be far advanced in his education as a polo pony.

The next point is to teach him to become accustomed to the ball, so that he will allow you to strike it in any direction you please from his back. Pony and rider will by this time necessarily be on excellent terms. The rider will know what the pony can do, and the pony will have entire confidence that his master will not hurt him. It must have occurred to everyone who has had to do with polo ponies that many of their faults come from a certain dread of the ball, or of the rider's efforts to strike it. Now a pony has three excellent reasons for this. First of all he is not infrequently struck by the ball. Some cases of this cannot be avoided, but I do not think players are sufficiently careful about it. The pony should not be used, as is sometimes done, to stop the ball, nor should a player so strike a ball that it must almost inevitably hit one of the ponies. I do not say this is deliberately done, but some players take chances rather freely. If the ball goes on, well, but if it does not, it is the fortune of war. The second reason why ponies dislike the ball is because they are often struck by the stick in the rider's endeavour to hit it. This too is an accident that sometimes occurs unavoidably, but again neither in the game nor in practice should our own or anyone else's pony be hit with the stick. Every effort should be made to avoid this. Every player feels justly mortified when he has hit his own pony, but some people seem to bear blows inflicted by themselves on other men's ponies with considerable equanimity. All polo players know, however, that many ponies are thus rendered more or less ball shy. I believe that this almost always arises from accidents and blows occurring during the early experiences of the game. If once a pony is fairly entered to polo and takes to the game, it is seldom indeed that they become ball shy afterwards.

A pony may show reluctance to go on to the ground, and yet play well when there. That is merely nervousness. I had a nervous country-bred mare when stationed on the Indian frontier at Dera Ismail Khan, that invariably reared up on being mounted before polo, but, once in the game, played like a book. For these reasons it is desirable to exercise the greatest care in the early lessons with the ball. Even if the pony shows no distaste of the ball from the very first, and I have known this to happen not infrequently, yet still the lessons should be continued steadily. The whole principle on which the system of training ponies here suggested is based is continual and steady practice, so that each of the actions necessary to the game shall become a second nature to the pony. It is not necessary then to say that, in training a pony to allow the ball to be hit from his back, the improvement of the player himself should be little thought of, and the whole attention given so to hit the ball as not to hurt the pony.

There is still a third cause of ball shyness in ponies. Some men have a habit of tightening their grip on the reins before they hit the ball. This is a vice in a player, and leads to vice in the pony. Every effort should be made to give no signal of what we are about to do to the pony's mouth. The rein ought always to be easily and lightly held, or, if that is a counsel of perfection, as we know it is with many players, then the same steady pull should be kept at all times. Theoretically, a polo pony plays best with not a slack rein, but just the lightest possible pressure on the bit. The bridle is a signal not an instrument of force. Yet we know in practice that many men partly hold on by the bridle, and that the check given to the pony at the moment of striking the ball is really for the purpose of steadying the rider in his seat. In counsels such as we are giving it is desirable to put a high standard before us, and indeed many men could learn to ride at polo without spoiling their ponies' mouths if they would pay attention to training themselves. But if, when you are schooling your pony to the use of the ball, you feel that such light handling is beyond you, at all events try to make the pressure even, so that the pony shall come to understand that a harder pull means 'stop.' Also watch the pony's mouth very carefully to see that you do not hurt it and make it sore.

The ground chosen for the first practice with the ball should be as smooth as possible. This is important both for the player and the pony. Some people have a theory that rough ground is a good thing. But rough ground obliges you to pull up constantly, and the great lesson to be learned is to go on hitting and galloping continuously. The better the match the less pulling up there will be, and what man and pony have to do in the game should be kept before the mind in practice. Several balls may be put down, each one being struck gently as we come within reach of it. This avoids the necessity of checking and turning, and is in accordance with the principle we have laid down of teaching one thing at a time. Very soon the pony will take no notice of the tap of the stick on the ball, although some nervous animals of course take longer than others, and some never do quite overcome this distrust of the ball. With the majority of ponies that have come into my hands untaught and untrained, there has not been little difficulty, nor have I ever heard from other people of much trouble in this matter.

Thus with a careful rider and reasonably sure hitter, the pony soon learns to take no notice of the ball. Men who can play polo at all, and keep themselves in steady and

Rose Stalk. The 1st prize, Islington, 1905. The property of the honourable Mrs Ives.

Rupert. Polo bred stallion, bred by Miss L. Standish. Winner of many prizes.

constant practice, can hit a ball about a field when there is no one to interfere with them. I have suggested above that whatever difficulties there may be between the pony and the ball come at first. It is probable that when once a pony is fairly entered to a game he recognises the part played in it by the ball, and learns to take an intelligent interest in its movements. Mr Moray Brown always declared that the ponies watched the course of the ball through the air and directed their movements accordingly. Everyone has known ponies that would turn at the sound of the stick on the ball, when a backhander is struck. One pony certainly always tried to keep the ball on her off side, and would swing with every bump of the ball, following its course, but always so that it was possible to hit when you reached it. This pony, which for a short time was in my possession, was by far the easiest to ride at polo I have ever been on.

I have now brought the pony from its entry into the stables of its trainer, up to the time when it is ready to go into its first game of polo. Everything after this depends on the player into whose hands it falls.

Up to this point any man who can ride, is able to hit a ball at a slow pace, and will take pains, can train a suitable pony. Indeed, I know several instances where ponies that now take a very high place among the best-playing ponies of the day, received their early training at the hands of men, one of whom was a most indifferent player and the other a very awkward horseman. If the trainer is also a good player he should have no difficulty in making his pony perform within the limits of its natural qualifications.

Of the best regimental teams, the 13th Hussars and the Durham Light Infantry won most of their victories on ponies trained in the regiment. The man with leisure will in every way find himself repaid by training his own pony.

In the first place his ponies will cost him less than half as much as if he bought them ready made. They will suit him better in all probability. The all round pony that fits every player is not common, and we shall in the end have fewer disappointments than will fall to our lot if we buy ponies that other people have made. But I am inclined to go a step farther and say, that I have seldom known a first-class player who did not train his own ponies to a great extent. Nor do I believe it is likely that a man will reach the first class on ponies in the education of which he has not had a considerable share. Nothing is more certain at polo than that the pony must suit the man and his style of play, and this no pony does as well as the one the player has trained for his own use. It would of course be too much to say that no one ever became a first-class player on ponies in whose education for polo he had not had some share. On the other hand, there are many instances of second-class players paying very large prices for polo ponies of reputation, yet some of them have never emerged from a very moderate class in the game.

I should not like to say that it is necessary to undertake the training of ponies from the first. Indeed, I think that the early training of the pony, provided he be in good and kindly hands, matters very little, so long as it has not been on a polo ground. If I were training ponies for sale I would make hacks of them, or even drive them in harness. They should be used to stick and ball, but they should never be played at polo, save possibly in a cantering game, until they pass into the hands of the man who really means to play them. It is often said by players that they would prefer not to buy a pony that had been in a moderate game, and I think that except for beginners, thoroughly made ponies are as a rule a mistake. I imagine that everyone could have played on 'Black Bella', or 'Little Fairy', or 'My Girl', or 'Siren', or 'Mademoiselle', or 'Yellowman', 'Piper', or 'Early Dawn', but on very few others. In fact, many ponies that are full of promise are ruined in these early matches and games. Men get excited, and so does the pony. There are many riders who are horsemen until they find themselves in a fast game. The pace of first-class polo is not merely faster in a single race for the ball, but is played throughout at a much higher speed than ordinary games. The man has enough to do to look after himself, and forgets to look after his pony; all his horsemanship vanishes, and the pony rapidly deteriorates. Many men bring first-rate ponies from country clubs to London, and wonder why they deteriorate so rapidly. But the fault is in the man. The pony wants a horseman on his back and finds he has only a butcher.

The best results are undoubtedly obtained where a player of high skill buys a pony that is a handy hack, or, if not too much knocked about, a clever hunter, and trains it in his own way. True, to do this he must be a horseman; but then I doubt if any man ever did reach the first rank at polo unless he was a horseman rather more skilful than ordinary. It does not follow from this that he need be a graceful rider, but he must have a firm seat and a light hand. The best players of our time, Mr John Watson, Col. Le Gallais, General Rimington, Mr Buckmaster, Major Gordon Renton, Mr A. Rawlinson, Mr F. M. Freake, are all notably fine riders, though in different styles. Messrs James Peat, Kenyon Stow, and Mildmay, among the older players, were examples of good horsemanship, and they are numbered among the finest players we have ever seen. Every one of these players more or less makes or made his own ponies. It is impossible to lay too much stress on the fact that even first-class polo is comparatively inexpensive to the man who trains his own ponies. Captain L. C. D. Jenner writes, 'I have a stud of six ponies; only one of these was a made pony when I bought it, and that was the only case in which I gave over £80. The rest cost from £60 to £80, and had never been in games before I bought them.'

But to sum up the whole matter. If we look at the facts of polo instead of theories, we shall see that to train your ponies is not only an economy but an advantage, and indeed that, on a pony fitted by your own training to your own style of play, you are more likely to come into the first-class games which it is the ambition of every player to join in. There is one more point to be considered. At what age can a pony be trained? We answer, that the age of a pony, provided it has not been spoilt by previous bad handling, is a matter of secondary importance. One case I know of, a pony which had been an ordinary ride-and-drive pony until it was sixteen years old. It was then trained to polo, and sold as a polo pony for £200, its previous value having been less than half that sum.

7
Elementary Polo

The question that will arise in the mind of every reader is 'How much of polo can I learn from a book?' Most of our leading players learned the game before any books were written. Nor can anything take the place of constant practice and the study of the methods of the best players. At the same time we can reduce the principles of polo to something like order, and give to the beginner a few useful hints to enable him to avoid errors and to make the most of his opportunities. That is the object of this chapter. I have aimed at simplicity and directness. For polo is from one point of view a more simple game than it looks to be. The difficulty and the charm of polo lie in the fact that everything must be done quickly. There is no other first-class game, except tennis and racquets, at which hand and eye must work together so accurately and with such rapidity as at polo.

It is therefore necessary that any system of preliminary practice should be simple and expressed in terms as direct as possible. I will suppose therefore that my counsels are directed to a young player who has a handy pony, is able to ride fairly well, and can command the use of a level field. In all polo books will be found advice as to the use of a wooden horse for practice, and Mr Withers has invented a most useful and ingenious machine. But the wooden horse has the objection that it requires the assistance of a boy to bowl and retrieve the balls, and in any case the value of these mechanical aids comes in at a later stage. No one could hope to do much who began polo on a wooden horse. The pony is as absolutely necessary to the beginner as the stick and ball. The pony must be one of those handy experienced little beasts of placid temper and considerable experience that are so useful, and one that will not be upset by the knocks which he will certainly receive. There is nothing for this purpose like an Argentine pony of medium size, about 14.1, that has had plenty of actual practice at polo. It is important that this first pony should be a sharp one, quick to start and apt to drop into his stride without hesitation or dwelling. He should also be easy to turn, and pleasant to ride.

Having bought the pony, and making quite sure that he suits you, i.e. that he is a pony you can do anything with, then proceed to test your riding.

Most people who begin polo go too quickly. They assume that they can ride, as indeed they can in a fashion, but after watching a great many players closely for years, I am convinced that the reason a certain number of men fail to make the progress they ought with the game, is because they cannot ride well enough.

Of course, many people would be very indignant if you told them this, nor indeed am I referring to the mere capacity for sticking on, but to more advanced skill in horsemanship. In my polo-manager days I used often to be puzzled by the failure of players to fulfil their early promise at the game. A man would arrive on the ground, introduce himself as a new member, and put his name down to play. Generally, before he reached this point, he had learned to hit the ball, and possibly played in a regimental game, or a cantering game at a county club. He very often showed great promise in members' games, and became marked out as a man who must be noted in a handicap tournament as a source of strength to a team, and be put down for a place in a match.

A help meet.

In the handicap tournament our promising new player
was a little disappointing. He played one or two strokes
astonishingly well, but on the whole his performance was
moderate. So it continued to be, and watching him carefully
you saw that he was always an uncertain quantity, with
indeed brief flashes of better play. Then you came to the
conclusion that these latter always took place when he was
riding one particular pony. You remember having heard
that, pleased with his own success, he had bought two well-
known ponies. They did not suit him and he could not
play on them, not because they are not excellent ponies
in the right hands, but because their new owner could
not ride well enough to make the best of them. Directly a
player of this kind mounts a new pony, or one that needs a
little bit of riding, he loses his form. It is in fact absolutely
necessary that a man should ride well enough to play polo
on a first- class pony, even if it needs some horsemanship.
Everyone who has been familiar with the polo of the last
thirty years will recognise the truth of this. How many men
have begun as promising players, continued as uncertain

ones, and ended by dropping down to the rank of those who play members' games contentedly from day to day, and only stick to polo because they find the clubs a pleasant summer afternoon resort? They play in the annual handicap and are defeated in the Novices' tournament every season. The reason of this is that they could not ride well enough. Pace and ponies have found out many an aspirant for polo. There are good ponies playing at polo, but the number of those that a bad rider cannot spoil (there are a few) is not great. On the contrary, I know men who would play well if they could find ponies to suit them, but they cannot, for they will spoil almost any pony they get on to.

There are, on the other hand, horsemen who can make most ponies play. Not that I believe that a first-rate and easy pony is not an advantage even to the best horseman it is. But there are many ponies first-rate but not easy. It is quite certain that horsemanship is the key to polo. I will not say that it is impossible to be a good player and an indifferent horseman, but when I turn over in my mind the names of the first-class players I have known, there do not seem to be any of the bad horsemen among them. I do not say there are no ungraceful riders, but that is not the same thing at all. Again, I can recollect several instances of men who were good horsemen, but who, either because they began polo late, or had not been well trained in games at school, did not at first distinguish themselves at polo, but afterwards, because they could ride well, became fit for first-class polo.

Next to want of horsemanship the greatest cause of failure is want of ponies sufficiently good. We all know players who would have been in the first class could they have mounted themselves suitably. Thus the would-be polo player is brought up at once by the question of horsemanship at polo. Perhaps the great secret of polo riding lies in knowing when to exercise force. It is quite certain that in the course of the game there are moments when we must be absolutely master of the pony's movements. We must stop and turn. Ponies vary a good deal in the amount of compulsion they require. The other secret is balance. Many men fail in this. In fact I think most English horsemen do so for want of a thorough and careful school training. But it is necessary at polo for our own safety and that of the pony. I have seen a badly balanced rider roll off his pony at polo, though he would not think of 'a voluntary' when riding over a country.

In the same way a badly balanced rider is likely to throw his pony down, and many falls do actually come from this. If you doubt the above you have nothing to do but to pick out a quiet pony, have a saddle put on, and make your man put a lunging rein on, then mount, tie your reins in a knot, and trot about without them. If you feel perfectly at ease and secure, well and good, but if not, something more is needed to complete your education as a horseman, for it is most desirable that the bridle at polo should only be used for its legitimate purpose of guiding or stopping the pony, and all the work should be done as far as possible with an easy, I will not say a slack, rein. How to learn? Well, I believe that a polo player would be immensely improved by a riding-school course. Cavalry soldiers are, on the average, better players than civilians, and less dependent on the honour of their ponies, because they have been through the school.

But there may not be a school at hand, nor, if there is, an instructor capable of teaching horsemanship. I will here give a few hints which may be useful. The first thing is to have a saddle that fits you, and it is desirable to be quite sure it is large enough. We think of fitting the saddle to the pony, but forget the rider: many saddles are too short. The weight of a saddle at polo is of no consequence compared with its comfort. If a pony could speak he would probably tell you that he would rather carry a few pounds more than have you rolling about because you cannot sit in the saddle with reasonable comfort. I think at polo plain flaps are desirable, and indeed cannot imagine any one playing with knee rolls. An old saddle is better than a new one, and stirrup leathers that have become flexible, than new and stiff ones. What we particularly want at polo are ease and flexibility of seat in the saddle. Therefore the next point is to learn to do without stirrups. The best way to be independent of stirrups is to ride without them. For some time in every day we should trot and canter with the stirrups crossed in front of the saddle. Instinctively we learn thus to sit in the saddle in the right way and to balance ourselves. What better opportunity can there be than now when you have a steady, easy-going pony with the smoothness and steadiness that are so desirable in a polo pony? Try this plan every day for a month, and you will see how strong your seat will become.

Having gained the power to ride without stirrups, the next thing is to do without the bridle. Put the lunging rein on and make your man lead you about until you can feel quite at ease without the reins. When this is done try riding without either reins or stirrups, then when you can trot and canter comfortably you will be far advanced in the style of horsemanship that a polo player should have. Of course there are always some people, who are quicker than others, but in any case these exercises will probably need to be continued for at least a month, perhaps longer, and there is no harm in repeating them at intervals. The kind of seat that a polo player should aim at is well described in the following passage. In order for the rider to be at his ease, he should sit well down in the saddle, without hanging on by his hands or gripping with his knees, which should grip only when occasion demands. By always gripping with the knees the rider is made to assume a cramped position on horseback. On the contrary, the seat should be maintained by balance and not by grip. When we use the leg we should use it from the knee to the heel. Fatigue of the muscles above the knee is caused by stiffness, and is a sign that the seat is bad.' These are golden words and should be taken to heart by every rider. These few precepts supplemented by constant practice in riding, which, after the first steps are taken, should be on as many different horses as possible, will do much for our skill at polo. The practice advised gives confidence, which is necessary to a polo player's riding. When he has become so perfect that he can as it were forget all about his pony, he has made a great step towards becoming a polo player. I am convinced that want of this self-discipline and training is the reason why so many players do not come on at the game as they might and ought to do. A man with a public-school and university training at games ought not to find polo difficult, and I may repeat what I have said before that horsemanship is the key to polo.

I am well aware that a man who plays regularly and often will improve in his riding, but the best advice to be given to a young player would be that he should acquire horsemanship, not merely 'sticking on', before he begins polo.

When once the rider is confident of his balance, or even before, since the two kinds of practice may well go on side by side, the beginner takes up the stick and ball. Indeed, since in the nature of things so long as the pony is the partner of his practice, he must necessarily limit his time out of consideration for the pony, it is well to have the polo stick often in his hand. Skill at polo as in every other game depends on judicious and painstaking practice. But the first thing that you have to do is to provide yourself with suitable polo sticks. Next to want of horsemanship and lack of suitable ponies, I am inclined to think that many polo players spoil their chances by not taking pains enough to fit themselves with polo sticks. The shooting man is careful about his gun, the coachman likes a whip to suit him, and the hog-hunter looks to the balance and length of his spears. Yet the polo stick is as important to success as the gun, and

more so than the whip or the spear. Choose your polo stick
with the same care as a trout fisherman does his rod, and
you will be rewarded. It is, however, impossible to lay down
rules about a stick. I can only say that you must go on trying
till you find the right length. I find that a favourite Indian
stick used for a 13.2 pony is 50 to 53 inches, whereas those
I used in England are 54. I am of medium height, 5 feet
10 inches, and I should say in England that from 50 to 56
inches would be about the variation in length. A big pony
naturally requires a longer stick. The handle should be
racket-shaped and bound with the broad tape we used to
call *newar* in India. I do not think that a loop is necessary
if the handle is of the right shape, but you can have one
if you fancy it. Personally I think them inconvenient and
possibly a little dangerous. The head of the stick, its shape,
its weight, and the angle, at which it is put on to the stick,
are all important matters. Some prefer the cigar-shaped
heads. I believe Mr John Watson always uses them, and
Captain D. St George Daly once told me that he thought
they would eventually oust the square head. The idea of
this shape is that it picks the ball better out of deep or
sodden ground, and it would be well to have some sticks
so made. The heads should be fairly heavy, not less than 10
oz., except for a man who uses a long stick and rides a tall
pony, when the weight, which can be greater with a short
stick than a long one, may be decreased. Other things being
equal, a heavy head gives more drive, and I should strongly
recommend young players to try a heavier head than they
have now. The great thing is to have a stick so fitted to the
hand and arm by weight and balance that it exactly fits.
If I may put it so, the stick should seem the natural one to
play polo with. At the same time, as your skill increases it is
advisable to see what changes you require. When you have
a stick that you like, take the weight of the head and the
length of the cane, and see that you have the others made

like them. It is very difficult to buy really first-rate canes in England, and a considerable number of sticks prove to be useless. India-rubber rings round the canes near the heads for about six or seven inches help to preserve them from splitting. It is the truest economy never to cease from buying sticks and trying changes till you have them exactly right. Thus, having a pony, and having learned to ride, and having provided yourself with a suitable stick, you may proceed to practise with the ball.

It used to be said in the early days of polo that practice at slow paces was useless because at polo everything had to be done at a gallop. But this we know now is a fallacy, that it is by steady work and practice at slow paces that mastery and control of the ball is to be obtained. Many beginners make a mistake in attempting too much. There are, if we think it over, about six comparatively simple strokes which, if once mastered, enable us to play the game. All the others are only variations of these, and come to us on the instant when galloping on the ball, but they cannot be reduced to rule. The chief thing for the beginner is to fix his mind on the simplest strokes and to master these. The rest will be learned as he goes on. The first, simplest, and most important stroke of all is to hit a ball forward in a direct line on the off-side of a galloping pony.

If it was possible for us to obtain perfection at this stroke, so that we could always be sure of driving the ball straight to the goal-posts whenever we had a clear front, we should have attained four-sixths of the elements of successful polo. All other strokes are forced on us as it were by the exigencies of the game. This one is invariably necessary and should always be used where possible. There may be players who are equally good on the near and off sides, but as a rule, and certainly for beginners in a game, the ball should never be hit on the near side if it can be reached from the off. That is, it is clearly better so to maneuver your pony on a twisting ball as to strike it on the off side as often as possible. One of the many advantages of a handy pony is that it enables you to hit the ball so much more often on the off side. Therefore, the first thing to do is to hit the ball straight forward at slow paces. Place a ball on the ground – and here let me note a little matter of detail not without importance to the beginner. The ball with which he practises should be a new one. It is all very well for the accomplished player to practise with chipped, shapeless balls. The beginner needs them new and round and firm. It is impossible to calculate on the result of a stroke on a broken ball. Besides, at the beginning you want everything in your favour. So take a new ball and drive it forward. Sit easily in the saddle, with the reins held firmly with a light pressure on the pony's mouth; grasp the stick firmly but lightly in the hand, quite at the top of the handle, and remember to hit with a straight arm. Do not try to hit the ball too hard, but rather to hit it fairly when it is rather in front of your foot. There is no particular spot in relation to the pony where the ball should be when you hit, for this depends on the pace you are going, the length of your arm, and the weight of the stick. But the two points to attend to first are: (a) not to bend the elbow, because when you come to fast play it is the straight arm that gives force to the blow, and a bent elbow leads to tipping or slicing the ball, about as bad faults as a player can have; (b) to hit the ball fairly and drive it straight forward. It is not necessary at this point to drive the ball far. It is necessary that it should travel in the direction you require. Thus, from a walk you go to a trot, from a trot to the gallop, obtaining pace from the speed of the pony rather than from the exertion of physical strength. The great point is to hit the ball clean and straight. This is a practice which ought never to be intermitted. As long as you play polo you can never have enough control over the ball at this simple forward stroke, on which so much success at polo depends. The next stroke of importance is the backhander. As it is the forward stroke that makes goals, so it is the backhander that saves them. The former is the principal stroke in attack, the latter in defence. Next in importance is the near-side forward stroke. This has been greatly developed by the modern game of passing and riding off. It shows how much the combined game has grown that this stroke has become more and more necessary, and as it requires a great deal of practice, the beginner, when once he can hit fairly forward on the off side, should spend a considerable part of his time on it. The great points to be observed in our early practice are to learn to hit with freedom, bringing the left shoulder well back, the back of your wrist outwards and, above all, to avoid striking the pony. It is better to miss the ball than to hit the pony. While the simple forward and back-hand strokes should always be practised from the back of a pony, the near-side strokes may at first be tried from the wooden horse. Many men find considerable difficulty in hitting the ball at all on the nearside and it is the first difficulty to be overcome. This can be learned better while stationary. It is a mistake at first to try to put much force into the near-side stroke. Whatever pace it has, will be given it by the speed we are riding when we come to do it at a gallop. The near-side backhander, though coming after the forward stroke in importance, is not so difficult. There are two other strokes which are indeed modifications of the four principal hits. And first, the stroke under the pony's neck across your front from right to left. This is, as any one will see who watches a game of polo, a most important stroke, for in our modern game when the course of the ball is, as so often happens, down the boards, it is by the use of this stroke that the ball is brought opposite the goal. The other stroke is from left to right from the near side. Needless to say, it is much more difficult. These two strokes are not primary strokes, but they are very important.

There are also two backhanders on the off and the near sides by which the ball is hit under the pony's tail. It is very evident that straight backhanders are seldom useful – the ball goes as often as not into the very midst of the players on the opposite side. It is generally advisable to hit the ball to one side or the other. To hit a near-side backhander under the pony's tail with any direction to speak of implies a very considerable amount of proficiency.

There are thus at polo eight strokes, four primary and four secondary, which everyone must strive to master before he can be considered as able to take his place in a match. These strokes are:

(a) Primary:
    1. Simple forward stroke on the off side.
    2. Simple backhander on the off side.
    3. Forward stroke on the near side.
    4. Backhand stroke on the near side.

(b) Secondary:
    1. Under the pony's neck from right to left front (off-side stroke).
    2. Under the pony's neck from left to right front (near-side stroke).
    3. Off-side backhander under the pony's tail.
    4. Near-side backhander under the pony's tail.

The forward stroke on the near side I consider to be the most difficult of all to reach perfection at. To my mind one of the most beautiful pieces of play that anyone could wish to see or a beginner can study, is Mr Buckmaster's near-side play. It is the perfection of ease, grace, and effectiveness combined. For style Mr Buckmaster, Captain Renton, and Mr R. Rawlinson stand alone. They not only make wonderful strokes, but they do them with astonishing ease and effectiveness.

Nothing can be more profitable to a young player than to study these players. Mr Buckmaster plays often, Captain Renton less than he did, while I fear Mr Rawlinson, seduced by motors, gives to petrol what was meant for polo.

All this preliminary practice needs much pains and time, but neither is wasted if spent in a thorough grounding in the elements of this or any other game. What the tub pair is to the university oarsman, or practice at the net is to the cricketer, that the wooden horse and the old pony at slow paces are to the polo player. Further, on the practice ground goals should always be put up and the beginner from the first accustom himself to register in his mind his relative position to them. The goal is the point to which he should always be making, and he should be able to estimate almost unconsciously his position relative to the posts. So, too, all the practice strokes should be regulated as though when going forward the goal was his object.

Another very useful elementary practice is goal-hitting. The ball should be aimed at the space between the posts at varying distances, from say five up to thirty yards. Once having shot at the goal the young polo player should never accept defeat, but go on firing from the same point or thereabouts until he has sent the ball through the posts. While practice is valuable it should not be too much prolonged. Stale and slovenly strokes are worse than none at all, and as soon as the player is tired he should leave off. This I think applies to every form of practice except the near-side stroke from the wooden horse, which should not be given up until the player has struck the ball to his satisfaction a given number of times. Here success depends on the flexibility of the muscles, and the combination of this with balance on the seat and a true aim at the ball. Constant repetition is the only way to obtain them. I need hardly point out that if two players are neighbours there is great benefit in practising together sometimes. But I am inclined to think that solitary practice is most beneficial, for a resolute man hammering away at difficult strokes is likely to be more successful by himself than in company with others.

From the very first, however, I should warn the beginner to avoid bad habits. There is the very bad habit to be seen in many otherwise excellent players of dwelling on a stroke. I wonder how many goals have been lost by this. A smart adversary just has time to crook the stick during that momentary pause and the chance is lost. The other fault to which I refer is that of snatching at or pulling the bridle. The best plan is when at practice to hook one finger in the breastplate of the standing martingale so as to keep the left hand in the right place. There are some minor hints that suggest themselves to me as I close this chapter, and the first is that while the length of the polo stick is best found from the pony's back, and is generally about as long as will enable you to swing the stick without touching the ground, the weight is best tested on the wooden horse. I have suggested that a heavy stick is an advantage and within certain limits one rather short than long. But the weight and the length are regulated by the fact that we have to hit near-side strokes. It is evident that if we only struck the ball from the off side and forward the stick might be shorter and heavier than could be used now. Therefore the weight and length must be such that the stick can be used freely on the near as well as the off side. Thus with horsemanship improved and a fair facility at the primary and secondary strokes, the beginner may think of taking his place in a match.

8

Tournament Polo and Team Play

When we come to consider the principles of polo for advanced players we are at once struck by the change that has passed over the methods of play, since the days when the counsel given to beginners was 'ride hard, hit hard, and keep your temper.' The practical effect of this was that the game of polo existed for the benefit of brilliant No. 2 players. It was in that position that the hard rider and hard hitter shone most, and the early ideas of combination consisted in making things easy for No. 2. No. 1 cleared the way for him. If No. 1 was not actually sent into the game without a stick, yet he was discouraged from hitting the ball, while Nos. 3 and 4 served the ball up to the fortunate youth at No. 2. The first team to treat No. 1 as a man and a brother was the 13th Hussars, and they were also among the first to show us the value of strong back play. We have seen the No. 4 of our polo teams rise from a goalkeeper into the most useful and important member of the team. We find him now riding close up to the game and going on with the ball when opportunity offers.

The best players of a few years ago were, with a few exceptions, forwards: Mr James Peat (1 and 2), the late Colonel Le Gallais (2), Mr Gerald Hardy, Lord Southampton (2), Colonel Malcolm Little (1 and 2) and Mr A. Rawlinson (1 and 2). Now almost all our finest players are 'backs.' There was, about 1895, a reaction against the predominance of the brilliant No. 2, and Mr Moray Brown in theory, and the 13th Hussars and Durham Light Infantry in practice, showed us the value of combination. Everyone then tried hard to keep in his appointed place and the polo player's motto became 'ride hard, hit hard, but keep your place.' All the books on polo described in detail the duties of each player in his place. Combination and order in polo were laid down as first principles of success. Then it was seen that combination might in some cases lead to sticky play, and that it needed in practice to be qualified by flexibility. Thus it is no longer possible in writing of the game of polo to divide out the duties as we used to do. We can no longer take the four players in order and lay down the functions of Nos. 1, 2, 3, 4, in any hard-and-fast way. A polo side in our modern English game has practically only two divisions, two forwards and two backs.

In first-class tournament polo we have travelled a very long way from the days when the rest of the side existed for the sake of No. 2. That player and No. 1 are nowadays practically interchangeable, and either of them hits the ball or rides off the opposing No. 3 or back as circumstances may require.

An additional obligation is now laid on forward players. They must not involve their side in the penalties for a foul. In the same way, though not to the same extent, Nos. 3 and 4 must be interchangeable. The tendency is for back to become the most important position. The modern rules favour him, and in the clearer perception we now have that in polo as in war the true defence of our own position is to attack the adversary, the back rides nearer to the game than he used to do, and goes up more and more frequently with the ball. He is in fact often the leader of the attack on the goal of the other side. Back will in the course of an ordinary game have more chances at the ball than anyone else. As the increase of skill in passing becomes more and more notable, the value of possession of the ball becomes greater, since if you once lose it you may not be able to regain it. Thus we can see that when the No. 4 having met the ball as it went back to the goal, is coming up into the game at a gallop and hitting well, it would be the wiser plan for the three men in front to devote themselves to clearing the way for him.

A little time ago the No. 3 was generally the best player in the team. Now I think there can be no doubt that the most skilful player should go back unless he is a weak hitter. If the best man in the team is No. 3 then No. 4 must try to pass the ball to him and run the chance of losing possession in doing so, whereas it is plain that the method of attack by which No. 4 comes up into the game and the others clear his way, is at once the simplest and most effective. But while the surest and hardest hitter should go back, the most trustworthy and loyal player, the man who plays invariably for his side, should be at No. 3. Within certain limits his character is more important than his skill. For he has to drop back or go forward as the case may require, in order to strengthen and sometimes relieve his back or support and encourage the forwards. Thus we see that in first-class polo the places in a strict sense are, like Euclid's definitions, only a theoretical foundation to base our tactics on.

The places at polo then are the foundation of the modern game. There are, on every side, four men whose duties are as follows: No. 1, mounted on a fast and handy pony, is supposed to watch the No. 4 of the opposite side, to clear the way for his own team by riding off the opposing back, and, while doing this with energy, not to commit his side to a foul by unnecessary violence and not to allow himself to be put offside. But No. 1, though he may not always find it his primary duty to hit the ball, is on no account to be so intent on worrying the opposing back as to neglect the favourable opportunities that will come in his way, not only of hitting the ball towards, but often through the goal-posts.

No. 1 should be a sure striker at the goal-posts. He will have to make up his mind often between conflicting duties, and decide for himself whether it is more necessary that he should be clearing the way or hitting the ball. For this no rules can be laid down, but if his No. 2 shouts 'leave it', he should do so at once, as the responsibility rests now on No. 2, who by saying 'leave it' has expressed his belief that he can either make a goal himself, or so improve the position of the ball with reference to the goal-posts that a score becomes more likely than it would have been had No. 1 gone on striking. Thus to hit or not to hit, to ride off or not to ride off, is a balance of probabilities which No. 1 has to be weighing in his own mind continually. There is no absolute rule, since the decision must depend on the relative position of the players, on his confidence in his own skill, and the pace, courage, and handiness of his pony. Polo is so quick a game, so rapid in all its changes that every player has to think for himself. The point to be considered is what is best for the side. If all players had equal skill, this point would be decided absolutely by the position of the players or of the ball. But the skill of players varies very much, and it is therefore clearly desirable, as a general principle, that the best player in a team should have possession of the ball whenever possible. Thus, if No. 1 is a sure and ready striker, it is better for him to take his opportunities, but if No. 2 is the better man, then probably it would be wiser to leave the ball and to ride off the man in front. A man who can ride off effectively is in reality less common than an average hitter, since riding off demands a combination of courage, horsemanship, and handy ponies not found every day. In attack No. 1 may have many chances, in defence the ball is going away from him; but a clever No. 1 can now shadow the opposite back most effectively and prevent many a successful backhander, or hinder his opposing No. 4 from placing or meeting the ball.

No. 2 is a player whose actions in the game must be governed by his knowledge of his pony's capacities. But his chief value, generally speaking, is in attack. When the goal is open to him and he has possession of the ball, he should make his way to the goal as fast as possible. That is not always as fast as the pony can go, but as hard as he can gallop without letting his pony out of his hand. No. 2 wants fast ponies because he needs to be able to go faster than the other players when his pony is actually, perhaps, at not more than three-quarter speed. If the pony is well in hand he will be able to regain control of the ball if it begins to bump and twist. It may be laid down that no man who has not perfect control of his pony can have control of the ball. Horsemanship, knowledge of pace, and a delicate touch on the pony's mouth have a great deal to do with control of the ball. Mere hard, wild hitting will not do his side much good. There are two points which No. 2 has to keep before him always: first, 'Can I take the responsibility of asking No. 1 to "leave it" for me?' Or second, 'Would it be better for me to ride on to the No. 3 or No. 4 and leave my No. 1 or No. 3 to go on with the ball?' If he is a horseman and has control of the ball, No. 2's great quality is dash. It is very pretty to see a first-rate No. 2, e.g. Mr G. A. Miller, pick the ball up at a gallop or literally snatch it out of a scrimmage, galloping hard all the time, and reaching away clear of the game with the ball flying in front of him, now hitting now steadying, and at last with one neat turn of the wrist' readying' the ball for the final stroke that shall send it through the posts.

The same quality that is dash in attack is quickness in defence. There is plenty then for No. 2 to do. He must be ready to turn at once if No. 3 serves the ball up to him, and to pounce on it and go away, or he must be equally keen to stop the No. 3 of the opposite side from serving the ball to his forwards. No. 2 is never off the strain. One of the secrets of his usefulness is a close unfailing attention to the game in all its phases, and a knowledge of the position of the ball and the whereabouts of the goalposts relatively to his own position. First-rate No. 2 players can never be very common. Good ponies, fine horsemanship, and unremitting attention to the business in hand, are not always, perhaps not often, combined in the same man.

No. 3 is a player who should combine the greatest knowledge of the game and its tactics with skill that can be relied upon. He may be called upon to take the place of the back and act on the defensive when that player goes up into the game. If the attack led by No. 4 fails, there is a critical moment for No. 3, for, if he fails to reach the ball, his opponents may sweep down on his undefended goal. No. 3 must be accurate and ready at backhanders on near and off-sides. At other times he must be ready, as Captain Neil Haig puts it, to feed his forwards, keeping the ball up to them and so placing it that his No. 2 shall have a chance to gallop away with it. His ponies must be handy, turning and twisting readily, and the position of No. 3 is such that he will not often have to gallop far in one direction. Assuming, as we may do, that in a tournament No. 3 is a player of experience and sufficient adroitness; his mental qualities of judgment, loyalty, and unselfishness are the most important qualifications for the place. He is often the captain, and not seldom the trainer of the team. He will not, perhaps, have as much applause as his fellows, but he will, if efficient, never find himself left out when first-class polo is to be played. A first-rate No. 3 can almost carry a moderate team to victory in spite of themselves.

No. 4 is now the most important place in the team. The rules favour him, his men depend on him, and the brunt of a hard match often rests on him. It is of all things necessary to the moral force of a team that they should have confidence in their No. 4. Directly the forwards distrust the back, as soon as they find he is allowing the ball to go past him, they are sure to go to pieces. Many a match has been won because the back has kept his goal like a rock, while the opposite side have worn out their strength and splintered their courage in attack. Then at last when the tired adversaries lose heart, and their combination breaks, No. 4 triumphantly turns defence into attack, and goal after goal is scored up to his side. So have we seen many a game won after the score had been adverse for forty minutes? The peculiar mixture of temper, accuracy, and quickness that are the qualities of a back, luckily rather improve with age, and when long practice at polo has given him a just confidence in his own skill. Like No. 3 he needs the handiest ponies, and quickness in striking off is most desirable for them.

He should be an adroit horseman, and able to handle his pony so as to neutralise the riding off tactics of No. 1, and to put that player offside by a judicious check of his bridle. In backhanders he must be perfect, not only those sharp strong clean blows that send the ball back, but backhanders delivered with such judgment that he can place the ball where he wishes.

It is worse than useless, at modern polo, to drive the ball right back among the enemy; if they gain possession, a team clever at passing may never let the ball go till they have scored. No. 4 must know when to backhand his ball, and when to turn with it, and go right up. If he is, as he ought to be, the surest hitter of his side, and can depend on his forwards, he will probably go right up into the game, perhaps through it, and find himself clear with at least one chance for the goal. If he has a just confidence in himself, when his own side are attacking he should not lie too far back, but sufficiently near to be able to meet the ball and send it forward to his own men as often as it comes back. Even in defence No. 4 should not be too far back, as if the ball fails to come up to him, the man behind may be able to hit it past him, and go on in possession to an undefended goal. He has often to reckon with lighter weights and faster ponies than his own, coming at full stretch before even the sharpest of ponies can have started. This is the outline of the theory of places at polo, and we see that it may be resolved into this, that given the amount of skill that entitles a man to play at polo in good company at all, No. 1 is chosen for his discretion, No. 2 for his dash, No. 3 for his resourcefulness, and No. 4 for self-confidence and if the self-confidence is misplaced, then we do not ask him again. Thus we see that the theory of polo is that there are four places with special duties assigned to each.

Yet very seldom in practice are all the four men in their own places at polo. It would be impossible to play our modern game unless the theory of places and their functions had been invented and elaborated. Nor is a player ever quite independent of his place; the duty of falling into it as opportunity offers keeps the team orderly. There can be no good polo unless the men have first learned to make keeping their places an object. This is true, no doubt, but the object of obedience to such rules as those of keeping your place is to enable you to disregard them at the right moment. Without the places the game would be a scramble, with every man making his place his first object the game would be sticky; and polo, if it is to hold its own, must always be now, as it has been at any time these two thousand years, a game of pace, dash, and resolution. We see, however, that the practical result of recent changes has been to increase the importance of the 'back.' The severer penalties, the better umpiring, and perhaps the fact that our very best players are verging on middle life, have all tended to make the No. 4 the leading man in the team. Another cause which has led to the same result is the increasing difficulty of finding effective No. 1 players, which is the reason in some degree for the practical interchangeability of Nos. 1 and 2 at the present time.

There are thus two forwards who are interchangeable, each one doing with all his might whatever his hand finds to do, wherever he may be placed. No first-class team would put any one player always in that place, except in first-class matches, inasmuch as continual No. 1 play spoils any pony in time, and the No. 1 must be well mounted. Probably the right place in practice games and second-class matches is to put the usual No. 1 at No. 3, and send the No. 3 to No. 1. The forwards are dependent on the support of No. 3 in attack, and he will be none the worse for keeping in practical touch with the duties of forward, while No. 1 will be steadied and his ponies benefited by practice at No. 3.

This would be equally true of No. 2 and No. 4, in as much as the former player must often in modern polo be in No. 1's place. He should be placed back in practice games, and No. 4 sent forward. The last named is often better for a little sharpening up. The objection to this latter plan is that a team should generally play with the same No. 4, so much depends on the confidence the other players feel in their 'back.'

The days have long gone by when back was chiefly a goalkeeper. He often leads the attack, and ultimately the success of the side depends on his skill in placing, and his rapidity and strength in hitting backhanders. The last point is important, and it cannot be denied that backs have a tendency to become slow and to dwell on their strokes, than which there is no more fatal fault. It is not necessary to be slow because you are sure. It is the quick backs like Mr Buckmaster and Mr L. Waterbury, Mr W. J. Drybrough, Captain Renton, Major-General Rimington, and Major Maclaren who win matches for their teams.

There is one point about polo that we must not forget. This is that in whatever position you are, the strokes are the same, therefore as far as practice on the ball is concerned; a man is gaining as much experience in one place as another.

It is not like putting a bowler on to bat, or even changing a man from the bow to the stroke side in an eight.

Thus we can see that combination, or as the Americans put it in their neat way, 'team-play,' is a most advisable thing. But it in no way diminishes the value of individual skill. As a matter of fact the most perfect combination serves a team very little unless they have one brilliant player among them as a sort of pivot for the team to turn on, and as a bond of union. Combination presupposes confidence, and this is greatly increased if all are sure of the skill of at least one player.

In several of the teams arranged for our matches against the American players, the men had combination without confidence, and were defeated accordingly. The value of confidence is shown by the extraordinary success of family teams. The Peats, the Waterburys, the Millers, the Nickalls, the Gilbeys, the Golds, the Grenfells, the de Las Casas, all occur to us without a minute's hesitation. The real secret of their success of course lies not in the relationship, but in the fact of the opportunities of practice together, and the Rugby teams are as effective with one or two brothers in it, because the members practise together continually, and thoroughly understand each other's play. Thus Rugby has in turn lost the services of the late Mr J. Drybrough, of Captain Gordon Renton, of Mr Freake, and are still able to hold their own in first-class polo, because of the admirable confidence in, and knowledge of, each other's play that exists.

Combination or team-play is of two kinds. If the members of a team are fairly equal in point of skill, the main object is so to pass the ball from one to another, that it shall be as much as possible in the possession of the side. If we may put it so, a well-disciplined side wins because they allow their adversaries to hit the ball so seldom, rather than because they are better strikers or it may be even as good.

Combination, however, has its limits, as we can see. To bring it to perfection it ought to be extended to the ponies as well as to the men. The men ought to ride ponies which suit them exactly, and ponies that are suitable to the places they are required for. But as a rule men must ride the animals they have. Only in a regiment or a county club like Rugby is it possible to pick and choose the ponies in this way. Perfect combination depends partly on handy ponies, and strictly speaking a regimental team being under control and having its ponies in common to a certain extent, ought to be able to beat any team that could be put into the field. But they cannot do so because a team of picked men, who have seldom or never played together before, would beat the finest combination in the world if the former were individually first-class players. An instance of this was seen in Dublin in 1895, when the Freebooters, a scratch team, brought together for the occasion, beat the most beautifully drilled regimental team that has ever been seen on a polo ground in England, that of the 13th Hussars, by 13 goals to 2. If we could picture a team perfect in tactics and combination, but moderate hitters, and suppose too that all the men were of equally good form and effective in any position, so that the team was practically interchangeable, I would venture to say that a scratch team which included such players as Mr Buckmaster, Mr Rawlinson, Mr George Miller, Mr F. Freake, would beat them as often as they played together.

It is quite true that combination at polo is a great matter, but it is by no means everything. Such play in second-class polo may easily become niggling and pottering. There will at times be some sparring to obtain possession of the ball, but polo must in the long run always be a free, open, hard-hitting, hard-galloping game. Sooner or later someone must make a run, and probably the side that has a man who can make brilliant runs and hit a fair proportion of goals at the end of them will win in the end.

I look with suspicion in the interests of polo on all attempts to reduce the element of dash and pace or chance, and, if any one likes to put it so, the substitution of the skill of a professional for the dash of the soldier. I am far from saying that this danger is near, but I think I see the tendency in the multiplication and increase of the severity of penalties. Even now we must remember that both in India and America the game is probably faster and freer than it is with us. But I must not be misunderstood to undervalue combination; if you cannot have brilliant play it is an excellent thing. The majority of players will always be men of moderate skill, and in close combination and perfect loyalty to their side is their best chance of playing good polo. And after all, perhaps it is not necessary that we should disturb ourselves. Human nature remains what it was, write we never so many books, and a man finding himself on a fast pony, and with a clear ground and fair confidence in his own skill, will contrive to gallop away with the ball when he sees the chance, nay, will even sometimes wait and hover a little for opportunities, or strive to make them if they do not occur.

The general effect then of the changes that are coming over English polo is to restrain the forward and stimulate and encourage the back play. While I am inclined to think that in India and in America the attack is still stronger than the defence, in England the reverse of this is the case. For everything in modern tournament polo turns on the defence. When the defence breaks down the game is lost. But the best defence of all is to keep the game near the adversaries 'goal. Therefore the modern back needs to be able to meet the ball certainly, to place the ball accurately, and to be quick.

The besetting failing of No. 4 players, as we have seen, is that they become slow and dwell on their strokes. If a steady and sure back has this failing he must keep farther out of the game than he otherwise would. It is certainly good tactics for a No. 4 to keep well up with the game if he is quick, and it is perhaps hardly needful to point out that No. 4 ponies must be sharp to turn and quick to start. It is far more important that the ponies ridden by No. 4 should have these qualities than that they should be extraordinarily fast. Also a back must be a strong hitter. The strong hitters generally make the best backs. Every first-class back of our time has been a tall man with a long reach, except Major Maclaren. The late Mr Drybrough, Mr John Watson, Captain Marjoribanks, General Rimington, Mr Buckmaster will all occur to every reader as instances of what I say. A weak hitter may succeed for a time, but he is bound to be beaten in the end by determined forwards. Weight is a certain advantage at polo both to the man and the pony, and of two teams that were fairly equal the heavy one would be the more likely to win. It is quite true, of course, that the Rugby team is now a light one. But I have before pointed out that the circumstances of the Rugby team, both as to their opportunities for practice and their choice of ponies, are quite exceptional. They only, among polo teams, unite the width of choice of a civilian with the advantages generally peculiar to a regimental team. They have always had moreover at least one superlatively good player, such as Captain Renton, the late Mr W. J. Drybrough, and Mr George Miller.

The ultimate object of polo is to hit the ball through the posts, and the greater the certainty with which a player can do this the more value he is to his side. Again, not merely the control of the ball, which enables the player to hit through the posts, but the hitting power by which he makes goals from a long distance off is most valuable. I have heard it contended that hard hitting is of no real value at polo, and this is so far true that if a player cannot hit the ball effectively when striking hard, he had better not try for more than he is able. But if other things are equal the hard-hitting teams will generally win, always provided that the control of the ball is not sacrificed to mere strength and power. Some of the great players who are noted for always trying to hit a goal if the posts are open and within distance of a shot, do not appear to strike hard, but they nevertheless make the ball travel far and fast. Such goal-hitters have been Mr James Peat, Mr T. Kennedy, Mr E. Kenyon Stow, Captain Gordon Renton, Mr Jack Drybrough, Mr John Watson, and Mr A. Rawlinson, the latter probably one of the finest and truest hard hitters that have ever been seen on a polo ground. Mr Rawlinson indeed seems to reverse the well-known saying of the old coachman, for what others do by artifice he sometimes achieves by strength. Another player who may be mentioned with these is Major Poore of the 7th Hussars, but he is seldom seen on English polo grounds. Hard hitting tends to keep a game fast, and polo would inevitably become slow if once players began to cease to put enough power into their strokes. Hard hitting is only likely to be successful combined with hard galloping. Indeed I think the former follows almost naturally on the latter. To hit hard and yet to retain control of the ball is the last thing achieved by the polo player, and can be reached in most cases only by the most careful and unremitting practice.

In the same way, perfection of combination can only be reached by practice, as we may see clearly by studying the methods of teams like Patiala, Rugby, the Durham Light Infantry, and the 13th Hussars, all of which reached their excellence in passing the ball by practice together. This of course is the point where many good teams fall short. It is only here and there that men have the opportunity for enough practice together to reach such perfection as the above named teams have shown. As polo clubs increase it will become more difficult to gather four of the best players in one team. The tournament team of the future will be rather of the type of the Old Cantabs, Magpies, and other similar associations of players where the men gather under the leadership of one first-rate player. This will so far affect the combination that the most effective team will be that which gives most opportunities to the great player. This will bring out again a further development, the art of leading a team. A good captain is as valuable to his side as he is rare. So uncommon are the necessary qualifications that most sides manage to do without it.

In an earlier chapter I have written on the desirability of individual practice in elementary polo. Constant work is just as necessary to the advanced player. The most useful strokes at polo are few, as we have seen, but they are not easy. There is one that the player must in these days add to the fundamental ones mentioned above. This belongs to the advanced game of which I am writing. I refer to meeting the ball. It is evident that if we can stop a ball coming towards our own goal, still more if we can send it back, the advantage is great. There is no doubt a risk, but this is much diminished by steady practice. Some years ago few men tried to meet the ball. The stroke was thought to be too risky. If the ball went past you while you were riding in the other direction, it was plain that some one of the adversaries might dash past and find the goal open to his attack. But with increasing skill and practice the stroke has become fairly frequent, and it is not seldom worth the much diminished risk which attends its use in the hands of a strong player. With the exception of Mr John Watson, who has never been equalled as a striker of backhanders, most players can place a ball with more certainty from a forward than a back stroke. In any case this stroke should be diligently practised by the advanced player. I said nothing about it in the chapter on elementary polo because it is not a beginner's stroke. This is a stroke which can be advantageously practised with the wooden horse which many players have, and which is provided in such clubs as Ranelagh and Roehampton.

I have come to doubt the value of the wooden horse for a beginner. But for a more advanced player it is invaluable. In the first place, a man in full play with a moderate stud of good ponies cannot well use them for all the practice he requires. And thus the wooden horse or one of the Withers polo machines is very useful. I am inclined to think however, that the ordinary shapeless block on four sticks is not sufficient. There should be something to represent a head and a tail. The existence on the real animal of these obstacles to freedom of use of the stick certainly affects our strokes, and we are apt on the wooden horse to indulge in strokes which would be quite impossible on a live pony. I cannot help thinking that it is the lack of realism in the wooden horse that occasions it to be less useful than it might. I think, too, that a saddle should be put on. The more nearly we can associate the conditions of our practice to the reality the better. The wooden horse is after all a substitute, and can neither entirely supply the place of, nor fulfil the same ends as, practice from a real pony.

There is one point more in tournament play too often passed over, and that is, condition in the player. If a man does not or will not keep himself fit, two things must happen if he plays in first-class polo, his play must be uncertain and he will injure his health. If we think that for a boat-race which occupies a quarter of an hour, we go into training for four or five weeks, it is absurd to think we can play a polo match twice a week without some care of our condition. Polo matches take an hour, and every muscle is exercised, the strain is great and can only be met by careful and regular diet and reasonably early hours.

If then we sum up the qualifications needed for tournament polo we should say that for the team is needed:

1. At least one brilliant player.
2. Combination.

3. Flexibility.
4. For the individual, besides a certain aptitude for games and at least some previous training.
5. Practice.
6. First-rate ponies.
7. Good condition.
8. Even temper.

Fortunately tournament play is not the whole, perhaps not even a very large part of polo. In the very nature of the game it is always an interesting one to play. First-class polo demands an expenditure of time and energy that not all men have to give. But, nevertheless, tournament polo ought to be the standard of every game, and if the full enjoyment is to be gained, everyone must do his very best, even in a members' game. One of the strong points of the ordinary game is its suitability for busy men, and the fact that we are never too old for it as long as we can ride and hit. What other recreation gives the same interest and an equal amount of exercise in so short a time as polo? It resembles hunting in this, that whether in the first flush of youth or in maturer age, it is always delightful and never palls.

9

Umpires and Referees

The recent revision of the rules of polo has made the umpire's position more important than it was, and much more difficult. Ten years ago the umpire in England had no power to act unless appealed to, and very little more in India. Now he must be ready to stop the game if he thinks the play is dangerous or unfair. A heavy responsibility rests on the umpire, for it must be remembered that on him depends the safety of the players. The pace and strain of modern polo is great. Play may easily become foul or dangerous in the excitement of the moment. The umpire therefore must be on the watch for the first signs of danger. But while he is always ready, yet he should interfere as little as possible. In all matches it is irritating to the players and in great contests to the spectators as well, to have the game stopped unnecessarily.

A breach of the rules must be obvious and flagrant before the umpire stops the game. He should of his own accord interfere only in cases of dangerous or unfair play. Thus it is clear that the umpire ought to pay close attention to the game. In order to be able to do this he must have keen sight and be very well mounted. An umpire's pony perhaps need not be very fast, but it ought to be as handy as possible.

If an umpire is appealed to he must make up his mind at once, and either shout 'go on' or blow his whistle without the least delay. Fouls or offside should never be given merely because they are claimed. The umpire himself must be satisfied that a breach of the rules has taken place. If there is but one umpire, however, he must use his judgment. That he cannot see everything is quite plain, and he must be guided by many considerations, the relative positions of the teams, and the character of the man who makes the claim. For this reason the Indian rules are right when they lay down that an umpire should be a polo player on the active list, who knows the men who are playing and can act accordingly. Now that penalties are numerous and severe, an umpire ought to be careful about inflicting them. He should be reluctant to do so. In theory there ought to be much care expended on the choice of an umpire. In practice it is necessary to take the man who will act. There is an increased tendency at the larger clubs for the polo managers to act as umpires, especially where there is only a single umpire to be obtained. This is probably the best arrangement. No one knows the players better than the polo manager, and no one has so much opportunity of watching their play. While he is umpiring he is gaining a knowledge of the relative form of the men which will be exceedingly useful to him. No one sees a game better than, or indeed half as well as, the umpire. The polo manager is a kind of official umpire, and our leading managers have all the qualifications needed. But there are times when it is undesirable for the manager to umpire. Then he must do the best he can and take any man who is willing to act. This often depends upon ponies, for an umpire will need at least two ponies for an ordinary match.

There are three kinds of men who should be avoided: the man who cannot make up his mind, the man who is always interfering, the man who will give his reasons. It has been very rightly laid down that players are not to discuss or dispute the decisions of the umpire. Such arguments over the rights or wrongs of the umpire's judgment are unseemly, and not seldom degenerate into disputes. At the same time an umpire must recollect that the matter lies very much in his own hands, and that he can do much to keep the peace by remaining judiciously reticent. As to any discussion of his judgments and decisions which may take place after the game is over, he must remember that a man who accepts a position of the kind is, and must be, subject to criticism. The great faults of umpires as a rule are ignorance of the rules of the game, which, however, they share with a great many players, and inattention to what is going on. Some umpires are never near enough to the game to see clearly what is happening. Others are never in the right place. Many umpires become so interested in the game that they forget to watch the play from the umpire's point of view, in which there should of course be a certain detachment. On the other hand, an umpire who keeps too near the game is always in the way. Therefore an umpire must have good sight as well as something of that trained power of observation which enables a man not only to see an occurrence but to apprehend it quickly. Polo is a game of quick happenings, and as men become more skilled, ponies better trained, and grounds more level, it will be even quicker than it is now. Thus the umpire needs to be a man of rapid apprehension.

But it may be said that in all this we have been moving too fast. Surely it might be objected that the first thing needful is for the umpire to know and reflect on the rules and to understand them. That is true, of course, but then every player ought to know the rules of the game he takes part in. The good umpire should have them at his finger-tips. He should discuss and think over the bearing of new rules and regulations as they are passed. There are certain points which an umpire has to interpret in the rules. The definition of offside for example is one about which there is a certain latitude. The purpose of the existing rule is to prevent a man from hanging back to snatch a run with the ball. A common use of the rule, however, which is a perfectly legitimate one, is for the back to endeavour to have No. 1 at a disadvantage by putting him offside. When the back is an adroit horseman on a handy pony this is comparatively easy, and perhaps is an unforeseen development. The umpire's true course is to be stricter in cases of hanging back, than when No. 1 is put offside for tactical purposes by No. 4. That is, he should require greater certainty that a breach of the rule had been committed in the second case than the first. In one case the benefit of the doubt would go to the defending, in the other to the attacking side. But if there is no doubt, then the strict wording of the rule must be followed irrespective of circumstances, and this in the end is the fairest plan.

The umpire should not be a thin-skinned man, or one with a pain in his temper. Polo is a very exciting game, and there are players who are more deficient in control of their tongues than of the ball. It is a gain when those players can be induced to umpire, whose knowledge of the game is such that people are unwilling to dispute or distrust their decisions.

There is a point on which umpires are now allowed a larger discretion than was formerly the case. They need not necessarily accept a cry for a new ball, if the ball in play is in their opinion sufficiently uninjured to go on. The probability is that umpires now will not stop the game at the cry of 'New ball!' when doing so would deprive the side in possession of a well-earned advantage. The fact that the ball is started from a point as near as possible to that on which the game was stopped, will not of course compensate for the loss of the advantage caused by exchanging a ball in motion for a stationary one.

Another point on which I have seen an umpire's discretion taxed is when a fall occurs. If a player falls off through his own fault without a very definite peck or stumble on the part of the pony, then the whistle should not be blown and the game stopped. 'I've fallen off', observed a player once to an umpire. 'Well, hadn't you better get up?' was the reply of the just but unsympathetic umpire.

In England it is not often necessary to order off the ground dangerous ponies or to warn players, but in India the case is different. Many serious accidents are caused by riding ponies not under control or improperly bitted. A polo pony, inasmuch as he is to be ridden with an easy rein, should always be rather more sharply bitted than a hunter or hack of a similar disposition, or than the same pony would be for the field or the road. In India, now that Arabs are so constantly ridden, the danger is less than it was when country-breds were generally used.

Umpires have also laid upon them the duty of keeping the game going. It is most important in London, where players are numerous and space is limited, that those who play should not overstep their appointed time, and the umpire is responsible for unnecessary delays.

There is another point on which the umpire would do well to be especially watchful. If the danger in India is from untrained ponies and sometimes, unless the nature of the subaltern has greatly changed, from reckless play, in England the chief peril is from the stick. It has always seemed to me to be the prevailing fault of many players, that they are very careless about the use of the stick. Umpires might, I think, check this more than they do. There have been at least three serious and many minor accidents from sticks in my experience. A word of warning to excitable or careless players would be useful, and if need be, the umpire's discretion in the matter of the use of sticks could be extended and his power added to in order to lessen and control this danger. In polo accidents will happen, and they cannot be provided against altogether, but it is possible to diminish the risks greatly.

Another point not without importance is that the umpires should be ready with their whistles. There should be no delay in stopping the game. Mr T. Drybrough suggested that the whistle should be carried on a wrist strap. Having found the difficulty of getting hold of a whistle attached to a cord, still more of one carried in a pocket, I think this plan would be a good one. Perhaps it would be even better if the whistle was fixed on to the top of a cane or whip after the fashion of the hammer-head of a hunting crop. This carried in the hand would be always ready for use.

The question has been raised if when there are two umpires, either should stop the game if he sees a foul, even if it does not take place on the part of the ground he is watching. It would seem to be right to give a foul whenever it is seen. The object of the umpire's presence is to check unfair play whenever and wherever he sees it. It has been said that one umpire should not contradict the other, and should not take evidence from the players, and this seems to be the best line of action. Nor should umpires discuss a point if they differ. The referee should at once be called in and each umpire should state his case clearly and briefly, and leave the decision to the referee.

The referee is, of course, off the ground, but he should have a seat reserved for him as near the middle of the pavilion as possible, and should be supplied with a field-glass. It need hardly be said it is desirable that he should follow the game attentively. There should be no difficulty in important matches in obtaining the services of an experienced player of note to occupy the position of referee. In the case of a tournament it is desirable that the same person should act as referee throughout the whole series of matches.

10

The Pony and Stable Management

The polo pony is an important topic, but one that need not delay us long. I adhere to the definition I have given in another book, that a polo pony should have hunter type and pony character. To that may be added the generous, courageous disposition which is one of the qualifications of a first-class pony. In the case of many of the best ponies it is not their make and shape nor their speed, so much as their docility and generous courage, which distinguish them. I look upon it as fortunate that the sire to which we owe so much in breeding polo ponies is a horse of a beautiful temper which he transmits to his descendants. Indeed, I have never seen or handled a bad-tempered 'Rosewater' colt or filly. As our principal polo pony studs are full of his blood, and the polo pony of the immediate future is likely to be of his stock, this is a fortunate circumstance.

As polo is played at present, a big pony is better than a little one if they are equally good in other ways. The rough bumping game knocks the heart and courage out of the smaller ponies, besides being dangerous for the rider. The preference for big ponies – and size we remember is in a horse not wholly a matter of inches – is very marked in the modern game. It is the result of experience, for a small light pony is certainly pleasanter to ride, and well-bred ponies could carry the weight of the ordinary polo player very well for ten minutes or less if it were not for the scrimmages. Weight, however, is an unquestioned advantage at polo, so much so that, other things being equal, the heavier team of the two is likely to win a match. I once read a suggestion that instead of being measured, ponies should be weighed, and if it was a practical one, as I think it is not, it certainly would give a truer idea of a pony's suitability for the game than any other plan. It is thus advisable to have a pony of substance.

Another point of importance is that the pony should suit the rider. So great is the necessity of this that I will try to illustrate my meaning. Supposing that a man was offered the choice of two ponies, one of which was a performer at the game of some note, and the other was unknown. At the same time, if he were told he might have only an hour's trial on the road, if after riding both, the unknown and inexperienced pony suited him in every way, while he did not quite get on with the other, then I believe the wiser plan would be to select the unknown performer at the game. No cleverness, speed, or other qualities in a pony are of any value if he does not suit the man who plays him. We like some horses much better to hunt on than others, but we can and do put up with horses that we do not like altogether, and ride across country with sufficient if moderate success. But with polo it is quite different. Every defect in the pony is a deduction from the effective skill of the player. I believe that the greatest of all defects is for a pony not to suit us. There have been many instances, some of which will occur to my readers, where a man buys a pony for its reputation at the game, with the result of destroying his own enjoyment of polo and diminishing the pony's value. If a pony suits us – and any experienced rider knows when he finds a horse in sympathy with him – we shall most likely have an animal on which we can play in our best form. In some cases the buyer can obtain a trial in a game, but this the seller is justified in refusing. Some men spoil your ponies for you by a single ride in a game, and if the pony does not quite suit them they crab him afterwards. A ride on the road, or a canter with stick and ball in a field, is as much trial as we can expect, and quite as much as it is wise to give. In most cases it is sufficient to tell us all that can be learned about a pony in a short time.

Having bought a new pony it is a mistake, unless we are very short of ponies, to take it straight into the game, however well trained the seller may say it is. If we ride the pony quietly for a few days and knock the ball about for an odd quarter of an hour until we are thoroughly accustomed to each other, many a pony will be found to suit us that might not otherwise do so. New acquaintances are often shy of each other, for a time at least, when a longer experience brings about a better understanding. As one of the secrets of success at polo is a perfect accord between horse and rider, it is worthwhile to take any pains to secure this from the first. It is, I think, quite as much a matter of pains as money. No one can be sure of going into the market, whatever his means may be, and buying four first-class ponies to suit him. It may be said that this has been done, for we see the fine teams of ponies bought at high prices by rich players on the polo ground. True, but how many ponies passed through the stables of these fortunate owners, and how much money was expended? You will never know, since it is not on such points that men are usually expansive.

Readiness of money and swiftness to seize an opportunity, some patience, and above all an unwavering resolution never to buy a pony that does not please us when we ride him, will in the end be the straightest path to success at polo. I may repeat here what I have said before, that for first-class polo the player must in every case put the final polish on the pony himself. Of course this does not apply to the ordinary man, who will do better with a thoroughly well-trained pony, provided only he can ride him with comfort.

The equipment of the pony is very simple. I should put the saddle first, for a really comfortable, well-fitting saddle makes a great difference in a man's play. A badly shaped saddle may easily spoil a good pony, so that from every point of view the saddle is most important. Next to the saddle is the bridle and the bit. The simplest is the best; an ordinary hunting double bridle is the most useful. The cheeks longer or shorter according as the pony catches hold when excited in the game. Fancy bits I dislike and distrust; I believe that if a pony will not go comfortably in a double bridle he is not much use at polo, and I am sure that nine men out of ten cannot ride him effectively at the game. Many ponies go better in a standing martingale, and its use is almost universal among those native princes and gentlemen of India who play the game. At the same time it must be remembered that foreign ponies, Arabs included, have not, as a rule, their heads and necks so well put on as our English ponies. Standing martingales are in fashion, but I see no advantage in them unless they are necessary. Nor do I see why a pony should not go well without a martingale if he is properly trained. It stands to reason that a pony if he has been taught to gallop properly and in collected form will do so more pleasantly with his head free. If a standing martingale is used, should we fasten it to the noseband or to the snaffle? The general opinion seems to be that to fix it to the noseband is the right plan. But in practice I have found it better on the snaffle rings, and I think we may infer that sometimes one method and sometimes another is right, according to the disposition of the pony. If a pony, owing to a faulty neck, requires to be strapped down tight, then I think perhaps the noseband is the better plan; but if, on the other hand, he may be allowed a considerable amount of freedom, then the rings of the snaffle may be preferable. In the latter case the pony is able to accommodate itself better to the pull, and by shifting its head to ease the strain on the mouth.

I should have the less hesitation in recommending a preference for the snaffle rings, if I was quite sure that the rider was sufficiently independent of his bridle to be able to avoid giving the pony unnecessary jerks with the reins. When once the pony will go comfortably in the martingale he would not need to have it on except when actually playing. Thus the risk of deadening the mouth would be lessened.

The Rugby polo boots for the pony should always be put on both for play and practice. They are one of the most useful inventions connected with the game, and save the ponies from many a blow and bruise that might produce lameness.

The stable management of the polo pony has for its object to keep the pony in hard condition, not only since he is thus able to do his work better, but also because he is less likely to suffer injury from or indeed to feel the blows and bruises which are incidental to polo. To this end a polo pony requires a great deal more of slow, long work on the road than he generally has. It is only by steady walking and trotting that we can obtain the condition necessary to enable a pony to stand the strain of a hard, galloping game. Polo is harder on the ponies than it used to be, and we must meet the change by improved condition.

Supposing that you do not want your ponies to ride or drive during the winter months, the best way to winter them is out in the open. A field with a shed in it is the best place for them. There is not the same objection to turning ponies out to grass in the winter that applies to doing this to hunters in the summer. The ground is not so hard, there are no flies, nor is there the lush growth of grass that makes horses fat and puffy. Now that the season is so long and tournaments so many, I think the first-class tournament pony greatly benefits by the complete rest of the fields. Of course the ponies should always be under the eye of a responsible person, and they must be fed regularly with hay and corn. This seems needless to say but for the fact that we know polo ponies are sometimes turned out and left to shift for themselves, merely to save labour and stable room. The polo pony wintering in the field requires careful looking after. His feet must be taken care of, the hind shoes being removed, and the front feet, unless very hard and sound, shod with tips. A pony's feet often grow very quickly, and they must be carefully watched. Another important point is a supply of pure water. Without this the ponies will not thrive.

As to taking the ponies up from grass and putting them into work, a good deal depends on circumstances. In some cases there is not stable room for the polo ponies until the hunters have gone into summer quarters. But where either there is no difficulty about space or labour, or where the polo pony is the first consideration, the sooner the ponies come up after the New Year the better. Most ponies are taken up not later than February. Take care the stables are not too hot. I hardly think they can be too cold. In fact, it may be said that no fairly well-built stable with half a dozen horses in it will ever be too cold. A polo pony unclipped needs no clothing at all when stabled, and even for a clipped pony one woollen rug is generally enough. Grooms are fond of clothing because it makes the coat look bright with a small amount of grooming. But this is not what we want for condition, for there is nothing so beneficial as plenty of grooming. Nevertheless we have to do with the world as it is, and to encounter the dislike of men to work, especially if they think that the same results can be achieved any other way with less trouble. Moreover, few stables keep a sufficient number of helpers to do without some artificial assistance. As to bedding, I prefer peat moss, for the following reasons. The animals do not eat it as they do straw, and ponies are often very keen feeders. There is less waste of hay. I used to notice that my horses bedded on peat moss ate up every blade of their allowance of hay. Lastly, I have never found any ill effects to the feet from peat moss if it be scraped away from the floor, and the pony made to stand on the bare floor for two hours or more every day. Indeed I am bound to say that with reasonable care I have had on the whole less trouble in that way with peat moss than with straw. I do not think, however, that there is any great saving of expense in its use in a small stable.

But the matter of most importance with polo ponies when once they are taken up is exercise. Nor is it easy to give them enough. It needs to be long, about ten miles a day. It should be slow, given at a walk or a trot, and it should be on the road whenever the roads are not absolutely frozen hard. For my own part I have no objection to driving a polo pony in harness, and I do not believe it does much if any harm. I have known some first-class ponies, like 'Skittles', that were excellent trappers, and I have a great belief in running in the lead of a tandem or team for conditioning a pony. Almost anything is better than the humdrum jog along the roads which most ponies have if they are left to grooms. However, a polo pony is so far better off than a hunter that he will probably have some variety in his work. By the middle or end of March, when a pony is beginning to come into condition and its legs are fairly hard with steady road work, a little work in the field or on the private polo ground will do most ponies good. Some there are that are so clever that they need no practice, but most ponies are none the worse at the beginning of each season for a little practice at figures of eight or other school exercises. The majority of ponies once broken to stick and ball take no notice of them afterwards, but I have known instances of ponies pretending they had never seen either before and that they were very much frightened of them. We say how stupid the pony is, but the chances are that it remembers some blow with stick or ball which we have forgotten, since it hurt the pony and not ourselves. In any case it is well to try them, unless they are well known and experienced favourites. As to the feeding of ponies in hard work, it is impossible to lay down rules as to the quantity. Some require more and some less, and each horse has his peculiarities, but if we take 10 lbs. of grain given in four feeds, 6 a.m., 11 a.m., 3 p.m., and about 9.30 p.m., or as near those hours as may be convenient, as a basis, we shall find that we are not far wrong. I have always used bran to mix with the grain, and believe in it, but it has the disadvantage of being expensive. I prefer long hay for horses and ponies in hard work, but in large stables the economy of the chaff-cutter is obvious. In small stables there is no gain in it. The best oats and old hay should be used during the polo season for tournament ponies.

The more experience I have the more firmly do I believe in leaving water always in the box or stall, but it must be changed often and the vessels kept clean. An ordinary zinc pail, placed in a ring fastened to the wall, is the best because the simplest plan. Easily emptied and cleaned, it is better than any permanent arrangement in the manger. The simpler the stable arrangements are the better. The best and healthiest stables I ever had were made out of a range of old farm buildings. The floors were laid with concrete and all moisture drained outside, the mangers were earthenware pans let into brick pillars built up in the corner, at the opposite corner an iron ring held the bucket. There was of course no hay-rack, and the ponies and horses had their hay as they ought to, off the ground. The cost of these boxes for eight ponies was very small. I may add that the walls were coloured with yellow wash, which is better than white. The stable doors faced south, and had each a half door, so that the ponies could look out. Horses may be very stupid animals, but like a great many dull people they are very fond of looking out of the window and seeing what is going on. We may be sure that they are not made any more stupid by doing so.

Polo grooms are very fond of washing their ponies after a game. It is a slovenly, lazy trick, and I would never allow it. Hand rubbing and strapping are most useful, and grooming is as important as good feeding to the well-being of a horse, if it be not more so.

EQUIPMENT OF THE PLAYER:

A kindly critic of one of my books in the *Spectator* accused me of evading the question of the dress of a sportsman by recommending a good tailor and bootmaker. I do not know that any better advice can be given. The cut of both breeches and boots is of so much more consequence than the material. It does not matter for polo at all events of what particular cloth breeches are made, or whether boots are black or brown, but it does matter that they fit well or ill. In a game like polo, which is played in public, the equipment should fit well and be smart, but it must be that kind of smartness which comes from the perfection of cut and workmanship. At the same time it should give to the player the utmost ease and freedom in the use of his limbs. Polo is a game which causes us to use almost every muscle of the body, and there should be no tightness or pinch anywhere. A really good tailor and bootmaker can do this for one without making breeches too large, or boots like buckets. A friend of mine, a master of hounds, considers that you ought to be able to draw your legs through your breeches without unbuttoning the buttons at the knee at all, and we know that Mr Jovey Jessop despised boot-jacks and kicked his boots off when he came home, but still in neither case could the garments have been either smart or elegant. Assuming then, after all, that we cannot escape from the tailor or bootmaker, white washing breeches, brown boots with straight, dummy spurs, are the right wear. Common prudence demands one of the polo caps which were invented by Mr Gerald Hardy, and are patented and made by Barnard of Jermyn Street. The cap is not only a protection to the head, but is the smartest head-dress you can wear. A polo whip, if your pony wants it, which I think but few ponies do that are worth much at the game, will complete the outfit. To this I may add that a counsel of wisdom and prudence always, but especially in hot weather, is to have a greatcoat ready to put on when we are heated with play and waiting for another turn at members' games or for a second match.

11

Polo Pony Breeding

The ponies discussed in this chapter come from four countries, Ireland, England, America, and Argentina. Of these the Irish and English are by common consent the best, and they supply us with examples of the stamp of pony which it is desired to breed for polo purposes. It is true, of course, in a sense, that you cannot breed a polo pony. But you can breed a pony which by conformation and blood is more likely than not to play polo if it is trained carefully and used with judgment. The object of this chapter is to show what is the purpose the breeder of ponies of the polo type sets before himself, to show why it is thought that he has reasonable prospects of success in his undertaking.

That we have the type clearly before us no one who will study these pictures can doubt. The problem to be solved is to breed ponies of the right stamp, and having done so, to fix the type so that the polo pony may take its place among our recognised breeds of horses in the same way as the hackney, the Shire horse, and the Hackney pony have already done. The first thing to do is to discover how the existing ponies have come into being, and, having so far as possible traced them to their origin, to inquire if it is possible by starting from the same point to produce similar animals. I begin with the axiom that, given time, patience, and judgment, you can, within certain limits, establish any variety of our domestic animals. You have, when once the type is fixed, to eliminate as far as possible the tendency to reversion which is the outcome of the law of heredity, so that your young stock shall come true to type.

Let us take the Irish pony, just because so many of our best polo ponies have come from Ireland, and because the origin of the Irish pony can be traced without much difficulty. Though it may be difficult to establish the pedigree of any particular animal, yet it is fairly well understood how the Irish pony came into existence. In the first instance, no doubt, they were misfits of hunter-breeding or reversions to smaller ancestors of that type. Before the days of polo, or at all events while the demand was still slack, but few Irish breeders intended to produce a 14.2 pony. A hunter was much more remunerative, or, if not a hunter, then a troop-horse or a trapper.

But at the foundation of all Irish horse-breeding was the pony blood of Connemara and Galway. Horse-breeding depends upon the existence in any country of the need for a working horse. The Irish farmer had and has a use for wiry, active, clean-legged mares of strong constitutions and even temper. They wanted horses that would work hard and live in the rough. But there was also in Ireland work for the smaller, cheaper, and hardier pony which could maintain itself on the moors and uplands. On these wild tracts of country there are great varieties of herbs and stunted shrubs, and these were just what a race of hardy ponies needed. Then these ponies were required for carrying burdens, and for such a purpose the peasants found it indispensable to have intelligent, docile animals – a sulky, stupid pony was no use to them. Therefore there was a continual process of selection for temper and docility going on. These animals became known, and their blood was diffused more or less through all the working horses of the country. There was, as in England so in Ireland, and on the borders of Wales, much pony blood crossed with thoroughbred blood. The mares so bred produced the famous Irish hunters which may be seen any day making light of the Badminton walls, crossing safely the Blackmore Vale doubles, or flying the blackthorn hedges of the shires. But now and again in the place of the big hunter came the 14.2 pony.

When polo began to prosper, these ponies were rescued from the slavery of the higgler's cart, played in some Irish county club, and coming to hand quickly, since an Irish man knows well how to school an Irish horse, they had a few brilliant days in the County Cup in Dublin. The best pony soon found his way to England, and when English condition and Irish horse-flesh combined had made him one of the best in England, came his day of triumph. It is the final of the Champion Cup or of the Inter-Regimental. The score stands at two all and but ten minutes more remain. 'Give me Brian,' says the master. 'He's had three tens already, sir,' replies the groom. 'Never mind, he never failed me yet,' and so once more the good brown pony goes out. Shrinking from no scrimmage and never hanging back in his stride, the rider's chance comes, and these two sweep down with a clear lead for the goal. Who whoop! and the bell rings. 'It's all your doing, old man,' says the master as he gives the pony a friendly smack and swings off to the pavilion, while 'Brian' is led away, his wide nostrils, his heaving flank, his quivering tail telling of the severity of the struggle. Yet tomorrow his eye will be as clear, his legs as cool and hard as ever, he will have cleaned out his manger and rested well. Let us see now what has gone to the making of this pony. First, there is the pony of the hills and moors finding his living on the scanty but nourishing grass and the fibrous stunted shrubs of the wild country of his birth. Then there is the struggle for existence which has developed his intelligence, hardened his constitution, and diminished his size. One of the chief factors in regulating the size of the horse is this struggle for existence. This is the reason why horses that live in herds are always smaller than those living separately or in small numbers. In proportion as we make life easier for the horse and lessen the stress of the struggle, or take it away altogether, does his size increase. Thirdly, we have, in the strains of our English pony, the working mares. The best polo ponies and hunters are those derived from mares which had real work to do, and Nature has given us a hint on which we should do well to ponder, that the pleasure of the sportsman has its roots far back in the necessities of the peasant farmer. From these working ancestors we have the docility and courage for which the ponies and mares have been selected for generations. Lastly, we have the infusion of thoroughbred blood, giving the speed and the shape and make which we need.

Speaking generally, we may say that, while make and shape, docility, intelligence, and speed are largely a matter of inheritance, endurance and hardiness are the result of climate, food, and the circumstances of the life of the ancestors.

Having thus analysed the materials that have gone to the making of a polo pony, we have to consider whether, by selecting the most suitable specimens of the ponies we have, we can breed with remunerative certainty an animal of which we can say, this is likely to make a polo pony if it falls into good hands. But here comes in a question which we are bound to face. Supposing that you buy mares of the right type and put them to similar and suitable stallions, that is, to horses which, while of the same general type as the mares, have those qualities which the mares lack, what security have you that you will not be disappointed by some unexpected reversion to some unsuspected ancestors? This may indeed occur, but what we have to consider is its probability. I think that while the existence of the possibility of reversion is not to be denied, its probability is much exaggerated. For this there are two reasons: First, that the general tendency of reversion where the crosses are not violent or to absolutely alien blood is to the average or mean type. This applies, I think, to those mental as well as physical characteristics, which can be inherited, and thus, of course, to size among others. Secondly, that the tendency to reversion diminishes when the races bred from are prepotent ones. That is, the tendency to reversion to a different type from that of the parents is diminished in direct proportion to the purity of the race. 'It is,' says Mr Vernon, 'when two distinct races are crossed that the tendency to reversion most often declares itself'. He goes on, 'The reversion of hybrids and mongrels to one of their pure parent forms after an interval of two or more generations is especially common. Hence it would seem that the act of crossing in itself gives an impulse to reversion.' The tendency to unexpected and undesirable reversion is then to be looked for less in the offspring of pure breeds, and especially of those which have been more or less closely inbred. Now, in the case of the polo pony, we have descent from two offshoots of a common stock, the Eastern horse, both of which offshoots have been closely inbred.

Let me illustrate this by the pedigree of a pony which is very likely hereafter to be selected as a brood mare. In 1904, a filly, a fine type of pony, named 'Modest Maiden,' was exhibited at the Knighton Show by the Radnorshire Polo and Riding Pony Stud Company. 'Modest Maiden' is by 'Shyboy,' by 'Rosewater,' by 'Rosicrucian.' The last named has four crosses of 'Orville' in his pedigree. 'Orville' has four crosses of the Darley Arabian, which please note. Now, turning to 'Modest Maiden's' dam, she was a Welsh pony by a trotting (not a Hackney) pony 'Royal Revenge II.' This pony goes back to Rystyk's 'Hambletonian,' said by Americans to be the king of trotting sires, and through him at last to the Darley Arabian again. Thus we have a common descent from one of the sources of our thoroughbred blood. The rest of 'Modest Maiden's blood is that of the Welsh mountain pony. Now all mountain and moorland breeds are very prepotent, because they are, by the nature of things, closely inbred. Alien crosses may from time to time be admitted, but such is the prepotency of a mountain-bred pony that they can absorb without much deterioration a great deal of alien blood. The climate and the food are always working with the inherited tendency to produce a particular type. Sir Richard Green Price tells me that 'Modest Maiden' is in foal to 'Schoolmaster.' This horse is by 'Wisdom' out of 'Brenta' by 'Parmesan.' 'Wisdom' has six crosses of 'Orville,' and 'Brenta' through 'Parmesan' has two crosses. Thus the chances of reversion in 'Modest Maiden's offspring would be very small. If, further, we carefully select for type, with each succeeding generation the chances of unwelcome reversion grow smaller, and the type we require a practical certainty. 'After six generations of selection,' writes Professor Pearson, quoted by Mr Vernon, 'the selected individuals will, without further selection, breed true to the selected type within nearly 1 per cent of its value.' We can then without undue temerity lay down that the polo pony of the future must be an animal containing thoroughbred and pony blood, and be bred from selected animals for six generations. In practice I do not believe so long a time will be required, for the above sample pedigree (and others would yield precisely similar results) shows that more than half the work is done for us when we begin. If, as is much to be hoped, the owners of other mountain breeds follow the example of Wales and establish stud books of their own, the task will be much simplified. Every Irish breeder knows the value of the old pony blood, and, as readers will already have inferred, English hunters and polo ponies owe their origin in a large number of cases to the Welsh or other mountain breeds.

Two-year-old fillies.

To those who doubt this I recommend the study of the Welsh Stud Book, which will be found at once amusing and instructive. For the Welsh Stud Book has the advantage of the vivid pen of Sir Richard Green Price, and the brilliant essays, full of wit and substance, of Mr Charles Coltman Rogers.

The above reflections will help us to realise two important truths. First, that it is possible to breed the class of riding pony we want, and secondly, that the mountain and moorland ponies are deserving of every assistance and encouragement which it is in our power to give them. What is needed is not any undue interference, still less crosses of alien blood, but a steady and sustained effort to preserve the purity and hardiness of the breeds. I should like to see the elimination, by law if necessary, of all diseased, weakly, or aged individuals, and the removal of unsound or immature stallions.

If horse-breeders are right in their opinion of the value of pony blood in hunters and cobs (and who can doubt it?), then the landowners and farmers of the countries where these breeds are produced are the guardians of a most valuable national asset. They should be assisted, encouraged, even, if necessary, with a little gentle compulsion, to do their duty by them.

The Polo and Riding Pony Society has done a great deal, and of late with the hearty co-operation of our leading polo players. Are not our best polo players among our best judges? and Hurlingham, Ranelagh, and Roehampton have thrown open their shows to the members of the Society, while Ranelagh in particular has striven to encourage the breeding classes by a liberal offer of prizes for brood-mares and stallions. The success of the Society has justified the policy of the Council in encouraging local effort. This has been achieved by granting medals and giving prizes at shows in different parts of the country. Moreover, members of the Council are frequently called upon to act as judges of pony classes and in these ways have helped to encourage the true type of pony all over the country.

But a more substantial stimulus to the breeder is to be found in the ready sale there is for ponies likely to make polo ponies. Four or five hundred of these are sold at Tattersall's every spring, and are all much of the same type. It so happens that the polo pony is the most generally useful horse there is. You cannot put him out of his place, and he will do everything from drawing a lawn-mower up to winning a race. The Government covets them for mounted-infantry cobs, for a trained polo pony is more than half a troop-horse already. I believe that we shall come to use animals of this type, not only for mounted infantry but for light cavalry. I sometimes dream of a crack corps of guides mounted on 14.2 polo ponies, and think how useful they would be. They should be officered by men who had all played in the Inter-Regimental Tournament.

But in any case there is now every reason to encourage us to breed polo ponies, or, if it is demanded we should put it that way, animals suitable for polo. The mares are always useful on and about a country house or farm, there is a plentiful choice of good stallions, and the market is a ready one. Prices, however, are not very satisfactory to the breeder. The breeding of the polo pony is attracting considerable interest, and the more largely it is undertaken the better will be the production of the raw material of polo, and the better will riding ponies pay the breeder. As long as ponies are scarce and the demand greatly exceeds the supply, the price of the trained pony will increase out of all proportion to the value of the untrained animal. We see this from the example of India, where polo has certainly not grown of late years as it ought to have done, because of the demand for trained ponies. If people will buy only those ponies that know their business, the dealers in Bombay or London find their business fall off and prices are lowered.

Major-General Haig, the present Inspector-General of Cavalry, has made some excellent suggestions. He advises that all ponies should be registered in two classes. Class A includes all those ponies that have never played in a tournament, Class B all those that have. He further advises that in inter-regimental tournaments eighteen ponies be allowed to each team – twelve from Class A and not more than six from Class B; but the whole number may be taken from Class A if it is preferred. The effect of this would be to oblige a regiment to buy two-thirds of its ponies when still untrained, it would increase the number of trained ponies on the market and thus in time lower the average price, while it would also stimulate the demand for untrained ponies and consequently raise their value.

Now it is clearly for the interest of polo players and breeders alike that the price of trained ponies should be lowered and that of untrained ones increased. At present the obstacle in the way of breeding ponies is the low price of the raw material. It is difficult to sell a four-year-old pony at all, and a five-year-old unmade pony is only worth ride-and-drives prices or a little over, says from £25 to £50, according to his quality. Some dealers do not make their ponies at all or at most put a finishing touch on them, and in consequence a polo pony passes through many hands, and the prices we hear of, which strike every tone as large, have had to supply four profits of which none at all went into the pocket of the breeder. A four-year-old pony bred on a farm represents an outlay of at least, £20, and perhaps more. Taking a very moderate estimate, a profit of £5 on this really only means that, one animal with another, the breeder makes no loss. But the following fact will show that this sum is about as much as the breeder gets as his share. Here is one. A bred a pony on his farm, at five years old he sold it to B for, £25. B played it at a local club and hunted it and sold it to C for £50. C passed it on to D for, £65, only keeping it a short time. D played the pony and, as it shaped well, sold it to one of the fashionable dealers for £50, who passed it on to a customer for £300 after playing it in several tournaments. Now this is not an isolated case. With some variations it occurs constantly, but it obviously affords insufficient encouragement to breeders.

The result is that we have a large importation of Argentine and American ponies, which are very good, but which have the effect of keeping down the price of untrained English ponies. If polo pony breeding is ever to be really successful, our polo governing bodies must turn their attention to encouraging the breeders. All that can be done directly the P. and R. P. S. do, by offering prizes and encouraging bending competitions to popularise the polo pony. What is wanted now is for polo players to turn their attention to encouraging the production of polo ponies. No way would be better than for players to undertake the training of their own ponies and by the adoption of some scheme similar to that recommended by Major-General Haig, but adapted to the circumstances of English polo.

It is quite true that we have succeeded in breeding ponies of polo type and showing them in saddle, as the four winners at Islington in the novice class of 1904 will make manifest, but all these ponies and most of the others coming on are in the hands of men of means. The P. and R. P. S. has been fortunate in falling under the control of men who made the objects of the Society their first aim, and with whom profit was only a secondary consideration. Such success as has been reached could only have been attained in this way. But the time has come when it is only common-sense to encourage others to follow the lines the Society has proved to be the right ones, and to seek a profit in so doing. That the future of polo greatly depends on the supply of ponies at reasonable prices being in some way equal to the demand, no one can doubt. If trained ponies came down to an average of about £150 and untrained ponies of promise rose to a price of from £40 to £60, the problem would be solved and one obstacle to the popularity of the game removed. There is a sufficient margin between the lower and higher prices named, to give ample profit to skill and judgment in selecting and making ponies.

The value of polo pony shows is unquestionably great, because there is no doubt that one great obstacle to the increase of polo pony breeding is that the farmers and others who might take this up with advantage have no real conception as to what a polo pony is. Many of the animals that one sees at shows in polo pony classes are quite unsuited for the game in any form. In the same way one is often shown with pride an animal that may be useful enough in its way, but could never be of the least good on the polo field. It is most important that judges should be selected who are acquainted with the true type needed for a polo pony. Judges who combine skill in the game with judgment are unquestionably the most suitable, and as a rule they should be left to handle their classes alone. At polo pony shows single-handed judging is the best. The judge has a type in his mind and adheres to it throughout, and supposing him to be competent, he not only gives as much satisfaction as any man can where there are but a limited number of prizes and a number of competitors, but his judgments are instructive to the onlookers.

These remarks apply only to classes for ponies likely to make polo ponies, and for made ponies. The latter class is not worth the money spent on it except in London, Liverpool, or large centres. In breeding classes two men, a polo player and a man who makes a specialty of breeding classes, one who has been a breeder but has retired, give the most satisfactory awards. In no case should there ever be three judges, since the best may often be outvoted.

Thus the game of polo has enriched the country with a new and most useful kind of horse, for peace or war. The polo pony is never out of his place. You can drive him, hack him, or hunt him, and he will do all these well. The possessor of good animals of this type need never stay at home for want of horses, if he wants to do any work a horse can help in, or enjoy any sport a horse can share.

Since writing the above I have read two important publications which support the view expressed in this chapter. It is not in accordance with the plan of this book to go deeply into the subject of breeding. I should like therefore to refer my readers – first, to the valuable preface to volume VIII of the *Polo and Riding Pony Stud Book*, written by Sir Richard Green Price. In these pages he sets forth clearly the descent of our polo pony stallions from 'Walton,' a grandson of 'Herod' (1758). The former inherited the notable staying power of his sire 'Sir Peter.' In the pedigree of 'Walton' the best Galloway blood of the period occurs repeatedly. Secondly, to Mr Theodore Cook's able and interesting *History of the English Turf*. The remarks (vol. II pp. 378 *et seqq.*) on the share of the English horse (before the importation of the most famous

Easterns) in the credit of founding our thoroughbred race will come home to every polo pony breeder.

'The old racing men (in the eighteenth century) were rewarded for their pertinacity in racing hard with the material they had, by suddenly discovering that this material crossed with the imported Eastern stock produced something much finer than either... What they already had in endurance they improved in speed, and what was fast was made to last as well.'

12

The Polo Club: Its Appliances and Expenses

This is necessarily a prosaic chapter, but it is on a very important topic. No doubt it will be the one to which polo managers will turn first. The care and improvement of the ground is the chief source of prosperity to the club. Not only is a rough ground very discouraging to playing members, but if your ground is a bad one it will be found difficult to induce visiting teams to come from a distance to play matches or to enter for tournaments. The type of a well-designed and well-equipped ground is that at the Ranelagh Club known to players as the 'old ground.' No pains or expense have been spared on it, and it has had the benefit of time. Ten years or more of steady work have done wonders for a ground that apart from its beautiful situation had not great natural advantages. When I first knew the ground there were some serious irregularities. These have been removed. The corner nearest the house was slippery and treacherous. This has been since re-laid. The club had to contend against severe drought during the two seasons I was most concerned with it. A dry season is worse for the grass of a polo ground than a wet one. Far more injury is done by galloping on a sun-baked surface of parched turf than by play on it in wet weather. A ground, it is true, looks dreadful after a hard match has been played in a rainy season. If, however, the treaders do their work well, replacing with the hand the clods of turf displaced by the hoofs of the ponies, and the turf is well rolled, scarcely a trace will remain on the following day, and no permanent injury of any kind will be done to the grass. In county clubs the polo ground has always the best-looking grass in the neighbourhood.

A polo ground may safely be used on three or four days a week in an ordinary season, but the same amount of play in hot rainless weather will cover the ground with dry bare patches. Where there is no appliance for watering the ground, a second ground would be very useful, but perhaps that is like the favourite prescription of the doctors to hard-worked people of nervous temperament and small means, 'Don't worry, and take a complete holiday'; most excellent but impracticable advice. A polo ground occupies about eleven acres, and it is not everywhere that a field of thirty acres or more of level grass can be procured, and this brings me to the question that confronts every polo manager.

THE CHOICE OF A GROUND:

In the case of a new club those who are entrusted with the first steps cannot take too much pains about this. The natural advantages which should be looked for are a level surface, sound old turf, and convenience of situation. If money was no object I should be inclined to place the last first. No polo club ever succeeds unless its playing members attend regularly, and my experience leads me to think that nothing in life is more safe to reckon on, than the dislike of mankind to inconvenience and trouble. As we have not only a polo ground to consider, but a polo club to keep up, we must have sufficient space. A polo ground should be as nearly 300 yards long as possible, after allowing for a margin beyond each goal of at least 40 yards between the back line and the nearest fence. Thus the polo field would require to be at least 380 yards in length. The breadth of a boarded ground is laid down by the Hurlingham rules at 160 yards. There should be a clear margin of 10 yards all round the ground outside the guards and boards with an added 40 yards at each goal end. These margins are most important, and rather than diminish them it is better, if necessary, to reduce the length and breadth of the part of the ground devoted to play. It is not only that the margin is necessary for safety but that a cramped ground is bad for both the players and their ponies. If there is a fence or other obstacle too close to the goals, ponies and riders will have a tendency to check their speed at the end of a run, and this spoils their play. When once the goal-posts open out before a player there should be nothing except these in his mind. A player galloping for the goal should, when he hits for the posts and believes he has succeeded in driving the ball between them, not therefore cease to gallop until the ball has actually rolled over the line. The same rule holds good for a man who is defending. The goal is never won or lost until the ball is over the line. Yet how often we see men pull up when they have hit for the posts, instead of following up the ball, and in the same way goals are often scored that might have been saved, on account of slackness in riding on the part of the defender. At all events no excuse should be given for this, but plenty of space allowed on every side.

Having found a field of sufficient size that is near enough to the centre of the district for the convenience of members the next point is to see that the surface is fairly level and thoroughly well drained. Nothing is worse than a swampy field. It is plain that a very uneven field is unsuitable, a slight slope or even moderate ups and downs are less objectionable, and where, as at Hurlingham, the centre of the ground is the highest point, and there is a slope away to either goal, it does not matter so much. The ground of the Household Cavalry at Datchet, of Eden Park, and of the Market Harborough Club, are excellent instances of fields

level by nature, which have needed nothing but proper care
of the grass to make them suitable for first-class polo. One
consideration, however, will limit the amount of rolling
done, and that is the cost of the labour. Mr T. Drybrough
has calculated that a horse drawing a four-foot roller will
have to travel about twenty-seven miles in order to roll
out a polo ground thoroughly. But we may take it that a
roller should be used as much as funds and weather will
permit. The horse should wear boots similar to those used
when lawns are being mowed. There are various ways of
top-dressing a field – bones, slag, and powdered earth. All,
however, are liable to sow undesired and unexpected weeds.
The simplest and most effectual of all is certainly to use
your mowing machine with the boxes off. This I learned
from Dr Hastings, and it is interesting to note that not
only does the cut grass make an admirable top dressing,
but that a considerable proportion, probably more than
half, of the blades take root downwards and spring up to
the great advantage of the turf. I do not think, however, it
is possible to lay down dogmatically any particular form
of top-dressing as universally applicable. This must depend
on the soil, the climate, and on the funds available. The
cheapest and simplest method of strengthening the turf is
to turn sheep on to the ground, never cattle or horses. In
the polo season the ground should depend on the care of
the club, and no one else should be allowed to interfere.
Nor is it desirable to turn sheep in on the off days. In the
case of London clubs where labour is plentiful, treaders-in
can be employed, and very useful they are, but the manager
and his groundman should always go over the ground in
order to assure themselves that the clods cut out by the
ponies' hoofs have been replaced carefully by hand, a
task the ordinary treader-in is apt to shirk. Plantain and
clover should be carefully extirpated; the latter is especially
dangerous as it makes a slippery surface.

There is one country polo ground where, in place of treaders, the squire employed the schoolboys to put back the clods before rolling. His wife soon received a request from the schoolmistress that the girls might be allowed to take a share of the work. Accordingly the girls were given a turn, with the utmost satisfaction to themselves and the club. Their neat little fingers replaced the turf most accurately, and it was unanimously voted that their work was admirable. I believe that sixpence a-head was the price paid in both cases. It is very light work, of course, and needing care and neatness more than anything else.

Not always, however, can we secure good strong turf, and it may be that we find the grass is foul with weeds and weak in growth. The best and simplest method then is to pen sheep on the ground in the winter, feeding them highly. In the spring put a harrow over the ground, then a chain harrow, and then roll thoroughly, and sow with some of the grass seeds supplied for recreation grounds by any good firm of seedsmen. After that, the ordinary cutting and rolling. A polo ground, however, repays the care expended on it, as everyone who has played on a well-kept ground knows. If I was forming a new club, I should also try to have room for gymkhanas without invading on the polo ground, and to have a space which would serve as a practice ground. It is desirable that members should be able to knock the ball about, and to try ponies, but it is most undesirable that they should be allowed to do these things on the match ground. I have referred to gymkhanas, and any provision for these will probably return the trouble and outlay expended on them.

The boards are a very important point in the outfit of the ground. The Americans call them the 'guards,' a convenient and appropriate name we might well adopt. The Hurlingham Club first introduced the boards, and they were found to improve the game. As originally introduced, the ball used to hang under the boards. Then at Ranelagh we adopted the plan of sloping the turf gently up to the boards on the inner side, so that the ball would not lie under the boards, but roll back to such a distance as would enable the player to hit it fairly with the mallet head. The boards are planks usually of about 20 feet in length, one inch wide, and eleven inches high. The top must be carefully rounded or it will cut the ponies, and I used occasionally to walk along the boards to see that the edges were smooth and that no frayed or splintered sections were to be found. The turf slope is made by cutting and raising the turf along the boards, and filling up with earth underneath until you have the turf within five inches or so of the top of the guards.

Then the turf should be carefully pressed down till there is between six and seven inches of board above the top of the slope. When the slope cracks away from the boards, as it will do in dry weather, a man should go round continually with a box or barrel of sifted earth and fill up the interstices. It will save much labour if the polo manager sees that this is done. My own experience is that the turf slope requires a good deal of care and attention to keep it in order. This is, however, one of the most necessary details in the care of a guarded ground.

Most clubs have a small lawn-mower to keep the grass short on the slopes. The Ranelagh Club was the first in London to adopt slopes, but the idea I believe originally came from Edinburgh. The boards of course are only along the sides of the parallelogram. The back and goal lines are marked out with white lime-wash by a tennis-marker. Care should be taken to see that the line is marked straight and that the goal-posts are exactly 24 feet apart. The paper goal-posts made at Willesden are the best I have ever seen, and the Ranelagh plan of standing them in zinc cases is most effective in preserving the posts. The new rules make it advisable to mark out a line at 30 yards, and again at 60 yards from the goal line or that line produced. For matches the centre of the ground may be marked, but in ordinary games managers and umpires should be careful not to throw in the ball always from the same spot, lest the middle of the ground be worn into bare and ugly patches. The ground having been thus marked out and brought into order, the next thing is to provide for the spectators, and for those players who are waiting their turn. Some kind of pavilion is desirable. Here I may refer my readers to the plan of the Ranelagh pavilion, drawn expressly for this book. It may not be possible to carry it out in every detail, but the study of it will be far more instructive than any amount of description.

When there is no particular reason for building a pavilion in any one situation, it should, as far as possible, be so arranged that the spectators should have their backs to the setting sun. I feel a difficulty in giving advice about the accommodation to be provided, because so much must depend on the expenditure possible. Two excellent small pavilions are those at Stansted (on the Silver Leys Ground) and at Eden Park. Liverpool has a very neat pavilion with tasteful surroundings. If there is a pavilion at all, there should be dressing rooms and bathrooms with hot and cold water laid on, if possible. In country clubs there might be a tea-tent for ladies, until a separate tearoom and possibly ladies' drawing-room, as at Roehampton, can be added. At Ranelagh the members' bathrooms have every comfort and luxury, including a shampooer always in attendance. But the best thing of all about the Ranelagh pavilion is that it has such a well-arranged front from which to see a first-rate polo match.

To the marking-board I have referred below. All that is now wanted is a bell to ring at the end of the periods, and in the pavilion a supply of umpires' whistles. Reversible waistcoats of red and blue, which are used to mark the sides, should also be kept. At one time it was difficult to induce the players to wear a distinctive mark, but now it is so great a convenience to themselves, as well as to the spectators, to see at a glance which side a player belongs to, that the jackets are readily accepted and worn. The Americans require the wearing of colours by the teams, as one of the rules of polo, and this is an excellent plan. But there is still one more requirement, which is of more importance to country clubs than to town ones. At Hurlingham and at Ranelagh where many of the ponies are stabled in or near the club grounds, and the trees are wide and spreading, there is no very great need for shelter; but in country clubs where people often come some distance, I think that there should be a few stalls and some shelter, however rough and simple, for carriages. Ours is an uncertain climate and something of the kind is necessary to the prosperity of the club, but this need not be a matter of great expense. Chairs for ladies, and little tables for tea, are sure to be wanted, especially on tournament or gymkhana days. As to servants, there must be at least one groundman to be responsible for the labour work, and a lad to help him. If you find an efficient man he is worth good pay. The lad is to mark the scores and ring the bell under

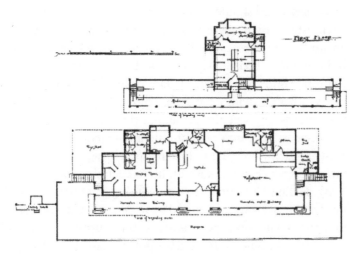

Plan of the Ranelagh polo pavilion.

the orders of the polo manager or secretary. This is the staff absolutely necessary to a polo ground.

In the present day when there are a large number of polo clubs springing up all over the country, and perhaps even more that would be founded if the fear of expense did not stand in the way, it may not be amiss to consider what expenses we can do without. After all the great thing is to play polo. Supposing that I were to start a club where every sixpence had to be considered, I should think over what was indispensable. There must be a field with space to lay out a polo ground. Mowing and rolling must be done, but an arrangement might be made with a neighbouring farmer, so that there need be no capital outlay for mowers, rollers, or horses. Tents might be pitched during the season, dressing-rooms or a portable house set up. Goal-posts there must be, but a blackboard and a bit of chalk will do for the score I think there should be guards if possible, but Cirencester manages to play a most excellent game and to train many good players without them. If the boards are objected to, either on account of the first cost or the upkeep, then the ground should be as nearly 300 yards by 200 as the circumstances will permit (see plan of 300 x 160 boarded ground). Of course, many of our best players learned in India without boards. Colonel De Lisle, Captain Gordon Renton, Major Maclaren, the late Colonel Le Gallais, and many others did so. I have already pointed out why it is that guards improve the game, but they cannot be said to be necessary. The expenses of individual members are their own affair, but I think a polo club often brings more money into a district than it takes out. It is sometimes said that the pony dealing element will be too strong in country clubs, but I do not see why this should be so. No one, with very few exceptions, who plays polo, is averse from turning an honest penny by his ponies. It is good for polo to have more ponies; it is good for farmers to make money whenever they can.

Nothing brings people together more than polo. Not even hunting is such a leveller, and nothing spreads horsemanship so effectually as learning to play polo. Anything that makes life in the country more interesting and attractive is a gain. Every club should, however, regard two expenses as indispensable, affiliation to the County Polo Association, and a visit from the Hurlingham official measurer. There is no greater mistake than to be careless about the height of ponies. Every pony that plays should have a Hurlingham certificate. To enforce this is no hardship on the individual owner, since it adds to the pony's value. I think many people regard the official measurer with unnecessary dread. Mr Sheather has no desire to reject a pony. On the contrary he regards it as his duty to measure a pony if he can. The rejections are wonderfully few in proportion to the number of ponies offered for measurement. People often think a pony will not measure when he is in fact well under height. The whole system of measuring and registration of ponies under Hurlingham rules has been made as fair as is possible. The more I study the question the more convinced I am that there is very little 'faking' done, and very little chance of its succeeding if attempted.

As to the amount of the subscription, that depends on several points, the rent of the ground, the amount of attention it requires, the number of players. The actual subscriptions for existing clubs, excepting Hurlingham and Ranelagh, which offer many other advantages besides polo, range from ten guineas at Roehampton (the last named club accepts soldiers at five guineas) down to two guineas at Worcester. Most polo clubs elect non-playing members at from a guinea to ten shillings a year. The subscription which will generally suffice for a country club is from, £3:33s to £5:55s for playing, and £1 for non-playing members. I find that out of thirty-five county clubs, five take ten guineas, three have a subscription under ten and above five, four have five guineas, three require four guineas, ten three guineas, and only nine demand entrance fees. But I think an annual subscription of three guineas with an entrance fee of one pound will be found enough in most cases. The original outlay will amount to about £150, and is generally met by a special subscription among the founders of the club. But it is difficult to lay down a hard and fast rule, for the expenses of polo clubs necessarily vary greatly.

In a first-class club in London they are heavy, the cost of labour alone making a very serious item in the annual balance sheet. The following figures may be taken as approximate estimates of the expenses of a London club. To keep the ground in order means an expenditure of about £200 a year, divided as follows: Labour on the ground for 12 months, £112; keep of a horse, £40; wear and tear of rollers, lawn-mowers, etc., £10; pavilion expenses during the season, £20; sundries, such as markers, whitening, renewal and repair of goal-posts, painting the boards, about, £10. In addition to this are the polo balls, a heavy expense. The cost of balls at one club for two grounds in constant use is from £66 to £100. The polo ball is made of willow root, and a year's supply should be ordered in advance. The balls when first they come from the makers are too green, and will be much more satisfactory if they are kept until they are thoroughly seasoned. I have said nothing about the expense of watering, which is, however, considerable, whether you have to pump the water on to the ground or it is laid on from the local water supply, as imperfect or partial watering, except a slight sprinkling to lay the dust, is worse than nothing. Where there are no means of watering the ground, the manager must trust to the rain. The ground benefits greatly by steady watering in the autumn months. When the soil is moist the earthworms do their work, and the roller should not be used immediately after rain. It makes the worm-casts into a paste which smothers the tender grasses. The common earthworm is indeed the most valuable ally of the polo manager. In the first place the holes he makes in the ground are a natural drainage and carry the surface water to the roots of the plants. Nor is this all, for if we allow the worm-casts to dry sufficiently to be brushed over the surface of the ground by a bush-harrow, we shall find that this is, in fact, the best possible top-dressing for the grass. The worm-casts contain an immense number of tiny seeds, a proportion of which sow themselves and strengthen the grass. That this is so is shown by an interesting experiment. A number of worm-casts were collected and placed in a shallow pan; in due course there was a miniature lawn made by the seeds which were in the worm-casts springing up. This of course applies equally to the ground which has the advantage of a supply of water and the means of pumping it on to the ground, and to those which are obliged to depend on the showers of rain. The use of the bush-harrow and the roller afterwards are the best means of strengthening the grass, and are far better than artificial top-dressing. The continual mowing and rolling to which a well-cared-for polo ground is subjected tend to destroy the coarser weeds, and preserve the short firm texture of the turf, by favouring in the struggle for existence the kinds which are most useful to us. But useful and simple as these methods of improving the ground are, they are not the only ones desirable. There are in almost every ground, until it has thoroughly matured by years of care and work on the lines suggested above, patches of weakly and unsatisfactory turf. These must, if possible, be cut out and re-laid. In a secluded corner of the park at Ranelagh there is a nursery for turf, where carefully tended grass forms a space from which the turf can be cut in order to relay polo grounds, croquet lawns, or golf greens. This grass reserve, sown with the best seeds and carefully tended, is a most valuable factor in the perfection of the grounds, lawns, and greens.

People often ask with what manure they shall improve their grass, but there is no manure which does not do harm as well as good, although in some cases it be necessary to use it. Nor is every dressing suited for every soil, but the water, the cutter (not a motor, they do not answer at present), the bush-harrow, and the earthworms will do all that is required in most cases, provided also that the grounds be carefully tended and the wounds of hard play carefully treated as suggested above.

We have glanced at the expenses of a first-class club. I now give those of a very well managed county club, the members of which play two or three times a week from May until September.

The annual subscription is £2:2s. for playing members, for non-playing 10s. 6d. The expenditure is rather under £100 a year. The secretary of this club has not counted the annual gymkhana meeting, as he points out that this cannot be regarded as a source of income; indeed, if the day happens to be wet there may be a loss instead of gain.

Perhaps, after all, a polo club depends for its success most of all upon its manager. How much Hurlingham, for example, has owed to its first polo managers, Sir Walter Smythe in the past, and to Major Egerton Green and Mr St. Quintin in the present, it would be difficult to say, and all over the country there are men who, by their enthusiasm manifested in real hard work, have made prosperous clubs. If it was not for the volunteer managers, polo would not be the prosperous game it is.

I have provided a picture of the scoring-board at Ranelagh, which is the most useful form of machine for that purpose. The names of the players are shown under the designation of the team or club which they represent. The clock face shows how long the match has been in progress, while the period being played and the state of the score can be seen at a glance. The scoring-machine being at the side of the pavilion is not visible to all the spectators. There should be a simpler board on the side opposite to the pavilion, showing in large figures the period being played and the state of the score. The convenience of this to spectators on a pavilion is very great, and if economy was an object, two blackboards and a piece of chalk might be made to serve the purpose. But in some form or another this second exhibition of the score should be used at every well-managed club, because it is obviously impossible so to place your scoring board that it shall be visible to everyone on the different sides.

Making a small beginning, and increasing its expenses and conveniences as the number of its members grows and its income enlarges, the small county club may in a few years become, like Catterick Bridge, or Fremington, or Cirencester, or the Blackmore Vale, centres of society and sport to the whole neighbourhood.

13
Thoughts and Suggestions on Handicapping

Few people will doubt that if a workable handicap could be devised a great benefit would accrue to English polo. That this feeling is widely spread is shown by the fact that several attempts have been made to arrive at a basis for a handicap. The old form of handicap tournaments in which men who wanted to play gave in their names to the polo manager of their club, who arranged them into teams such as in his judgment would give the best results, was all very well while polo players were a comparatively small body. Most of the men were known to each other and to the manager. If he was a judge of the game there was a fair chance of interesting and well-contested matches being arranged. Even then the most careful calculations were often upset. Sometimes a strong player either could not or would not do his best in moderate company, at other times an ordinary player manifested unexpectedly good form under the stimulus of a tournament. Even if the first round provided some fairly close matches, everything was apt to fall into confusion by the time the second ties came to be played off. Polo players are not all men of leisure, and it is sometimes impossible to collect the teams at the time appointed. Trial and handicap tournaments are often uninteresting, because, for one reason, there is no satisfactory way of filling up unavoidable vacancies in the competing teams. If, however, there was a handicap, it would be easy to call in another player of equal handicap value. Again, polo players are far more numerous than they were, and the polo manager cannot always have a minute and accurate estimate of the play of the men entered for a club handicap tournament. Some may be unknown to him; others may be newly elected members who have hitherto only played in their county club. There is therefore only a languid interest felt in these so-called handicap tournaments, even by those who play in them.

Another rough method of handicapping is to make it a condition that not more than one or two men, who have played in the finals of certain tournaments, are allowed in any one team that is entered for the tournament. But there are many chances at polo. The best team may be beaten, and the runners-up may be in their position rather by fortune than play. So that the very men who ought to play in second-class tournaments will be excluded.

Then there is the Recent Form List, which is published annually by the Hurlingham Club. The need that is felt for a handicap is shown by the fact that this Recent Form List was proposed, and has been kept in its place by the influence of the County Polo Association, in spite of the dislike with which it is regarded by many people. The defects of this plan of an official list of men who are to be barred from playing in certain tournaments are obvious. If all were equal in skill at the game it might be all very well, but they are not, as an attempt to handicap would show, or a glance at the specimen handicap in this chapter will illustrate. The Recent Form List is rather an expedient to avoid the necessity of facing the handicap question than a real solution of the difficulty. That it has some obvious disadvantages every one can see, and it is inherently faulty because it proceeds on the principle of excluding players, whereas the true handicap should enable us to include as many as possible. What we want then is a handicap which shall enable first- and second-class teams to contend against one another with some prospect of making a fight of it; secondly, to afford a convenient method for the classification and variation of tournaments.

I have long felt that sooner or later a handicap would be necessary. In order the better to record the play at Hurlingham and Ranelagh, and to avoid hasty and inaccurate judgments, I have for long kept a private handicap book, which I began when polo manager at the Ranelagh Club, so as to be able to arrange the games on sound principles. After testing and rejecting various methods, the only workable scheme I could find was to adopt with some modification the American plan of expressing the handicap value of each player in terms of goals; this must be modified in the case of English polo players, by the fact that the close team-playing or combination makes a man of greater value to one particular team than to any other. In addition to this the question of ponies has to be considered, and to this I shall refer presently, as far as it modifies the handicap.

The plan then is as follows. Each man might be given a number in an official handicap book at Hurlingham. The expression 'handicap number' is perhaps better than 'goals,' but the matter is not of great consequence. The highest number is ten, the lowest two. It is plain that there will always be a certain number of players who are below the handicap standard. No man, however, need be included in the handicap unless he has played a given number of times in a recognised team, and perhaps in certain tournaments. Conversely, no player not handicapped would be permitted to play in the teams and tournaments specified. It would thus become the object of every player to qualify for a number in the handicap book, and this would be a stimulus to improvement. Incidentally the handicap would give the governing body of the game a considerable disciplinary power, since to be struck out of the handicap book would exclude a player from first-class polo.

While the handicap would be arranged and controlled by the Hurlingham Polo Committee, or persons appointed by that body, it would be open to the stewards of any recognised tournament to modify the aggregate handicaps of any team competing in tournaments under their control, provided they did so with the consent of the official handicappers. Moreover, such stewards would be allowed to admit their own members to play in a handicap tournament even though their members were not handicapped in the book, such members not having a higher number than two assigned to them, all numbers higher than two being under the control of the official handicappers. In the case of county club handicaps the managers would publish the names of the teams entered, with their handicaps, a week before the tournament, so that teams could accept or not as they thought fit.

There would, of course, be nothing to prevent county clubs having their own handicaps, provided that, for the tournaments under Hurlingham handicap rules, only men in the official handicap book should compete.

I propose now to give examples of what I mean by reference to my handicap book. It will be understood that the handicap numbers suggested have no pretension to authority, or to do more than indicate roughly for the purposes of this chapter the handicap values. These are tested by a certain number of matches taken at random from the principal contests of the last few years. I take these from a much larger number of examples I have used to test my private handicap. The numbers opposite the names are the result of the following method. A rough handicap being made as basis after each day's play, I compared the actual scores with what they ought to have been if my handicap was approximately correct. If it worked out fairly well in a considerable number of instances, I allowed the handicap to stand. If not, I tried to discover by careful study of the play where it was wrong, and why. In the course of these tests it became plain that certain players were always much more effective as members of particular combinations than of others.

This difficulty may be met by a kind of sliding scale for some players. Taking their highest possible number, that which they were worth with some particular team, one or more points are subtracted from their number when they are playing with other teams. In order to make my meaning clear, I have added here a specimen handicap of the players (with a few additions and omissions) who were picked out by Captain Miller and the Hurlingham Club to form their respective lists of first-class players. First, I give the list with the handicap number. Then a few matches which were all actually played, with date and place given, to show how the handicap works. Many of my readers will no doubt find fault with the handicap, and think that they could have made a much better one. No doubt they could. But it is the object of this chapter to turn men's minds to the subject of the handicap. My end will be sufficiently attained if I can show its necessity. If an approximate handicap can be produced by a person of moderate intelligence, then greater minds having turned their attention to it, we could have a very correct and useful piece of work indeed. The object I aim at is very far from even suggesting that the following handicap is a good one, but to show that if I have succeeded in producing an approximate handicap, how much more could a sub-committee of any recognised club produce a really working list. I wish further to suggest that while the players in question, by a rough classification, may be regarded as no doubt in the first class, yet that there are considerable differences in their value to a team. I am quite aware that the expression 'first-class' player has no official sanction. But it expresses a fact, and is generally used and understood; therefore it serves well enough here.

In offering some examples, I may say that when I have not handicapped a player in my list, and the name occurs in one of the matches, his handicap number is taken from my book. In all cases the handicap allowance is subtracted from the total number of goals made by the side having the higher aggregate. When the number to be subtracted is higher than the goals actually made, the additional goal is not counted, e.g. A team has a higher aggregate than B team by five goals. They play a match, A makes four goals, B one. Then 4-5 = -1. B wins, but is not credited with more than one goal. The principle being that in a handicap match you win or lose the score after that being of no value.

The test to which the handicap is subjected is that, if it is correct, a reasonable number of matches now won by the stronger team would fall to the weaker, or the scores would be brought almost on to an equality. I have chosen fairly recent matches from well-known tournaments and notable players for examples, because every reader can judge of the value of the calculations more readily in this way. If fairly tested, I believe, however, the system would work out well. At all events here are the examples chosen on the above-named grounds from the many by which I have tested the plan:

	Handicaps	
Name	*Number*	*Remarks*
Mr W. Buckmaster	10	
Mr A. Rawlinson	8	
Mr G. Miller	8	
Mr F. Freake	7	
Captain Miller	7	
Captain H. Lloyd	6	
Mr P. Nickalls	6	

Mr M. Nickalls	6	
Captain Haig	6	
Captain Heseltine	6	
Mr F. Gill	6	
Captain Jenner	6	
Mr C. Nickalls	5	
Mr Scott Robson	5	
Captain Marjoribanks	5	with Rugby
	4	other teams
Lord Shrewsbury	5	with Rugby
	4	other teams
Mr C. D. Miller	5	with Rugby
	4	other teams
Mr W. Jones	5	
Captain H. Wilson	4	
Mr E. B. Sheppard	4	
Mr F. Hargreaves	4	
Mr Thynne	4	
Mr H. Rich	4	
Mr E. Brassey	4	
Mr H. Brassey	4	with Old Cantabs
	3	other teams
Mr W. M'Creery	3	
Mr L. M'Creery	3	
Mr F. Menzies	3	
Mr H. Brassey	3	
Mr Ellison	3	
Captain Harman	3	
Captain Lannowe	3	

Example 1

Champion Cup of 1903

Ranelagh	*v.*	Magpies	
Mr M. de Las Casas	3	Capt M Lannowe	3
Capt Harman	3	Col De Lisle	5
Mr F. A. Gill	6	Capt Lloyd	6
Mr A.de Las Casas	4	Mr Thynne	4
	16		18

Final score: Magpies, 3; Ranelagh, 1
Handicap, 3-2 = 1 makes the teams level.

Example 2

Champion Cup of 1903

Rugby	*v.*	Old Cantabs	
Mr W. Jones	5	Mr W. M'Creery	4
Mr G. Miller	9	Mr F. Freake	7
Capt. E Miller	7	Capt. Heseltine	6
Mr C. Miller	5	Mr L. M'Creery	3
	26		20

Final score: Rugby,6; Old Cantabs, 1.
Handicap: Rugby, 6-6 = 0. Old Cantabs win.

Example 3

Champion Cup of 1903

Rugby	*v.*	Old Oxonians	
Mr W. Jones	5	Mr C. Nickalls	5
Mr G. Miller	8	Mr M. Nickalls	6
Capt E. D. Miller	7	Mr P. Nickalls	6
Mr C. D. Miller	5	Mr H. Brassey	4
	25		21

Here the handicap works well. Rugby were better mounted.
The scores were:

Rugby, 4; Old Oxonians, 1. Handicap, 4-4 = 0. Old
Oxonians won.

Example 4

Played at Hurlingham, May 9th 1903

Mulgrave House	*v.*	Roehampton	
Capt. Heseltine	6	Mr F. Grenfell	2
Capt. Jenner	5	Mr H. Wilson	5
Major Egerton Green	4	Capt. Miller	7
Mr Thynne	4	Mr Ezra	3
	19		17

Final score: Roehampton, 6; Mulgrave House, 3.
Roehampton wins.

Example 5

Social Clubs Tournament, May 9th

Turf	*v.*	White's	
Capt. R. Ward	4	Lord Shrewsbury	4
Mr H. Brassey	3	Mr G. Miller	9
Mr F. Menzies	3	Mr P. Nickalls	7
Mr Marjoribanks	5	Mr C. Miller	3
	15		23

Final score: White's, 6; Turf, 4.

In this case the handicap would have enabled the weaker team to win.

White's was practically a Rugby team, all the players were throughly accustomed to each other's play, and they were probably better mounted than their opponents.

Example 6

Played at Roehampton

Ranelagh	*v.*	Roehampton	
Capt. Holland	2	Mr Horlick	2
Major Vaughan	6	Mr Jones	4
Mr Gill	6	Mr G. A. Miller	
Capt. Haig	6	Mr W. Buckmaster	
	20		24

Final score: Roehampton, 6; Ranelagh, 3.

Under handicap 6-4 = 2 Ranelagh wins.

Example 7

Rugby	*v.*	Old Oxonians	
Same team and handicap as in example 3		Mr Astor	3
		Mr M. Nickalls	6
		Mr C. Nickalls	5
		Mr P. Nickalls	6
	25		20

Final score: Rugby 3; Old Oxon., 2.

Old Oxon. wins under handicap.

Example 8

At Roehampton on June 6th 1904

Rugby	*v.*	Roehampton	
Mr W. Jones	5	H. Schwind	2
Earl of Shrewsbury	5	F. Menzies	3
Captain E. D. Miller	7	C. P. Nickalls	5
Mr C. D. Miller	5	H. Scott Robson	5
	22		15

Final score: Rugby, 7; Roehampton, 3.

Under handicap 7-7 = 0 Roehampton wins.

Example 9

Open Cup, Ranelagh, June 20

Rugby	*v.*	Ranelagh	
W. Jones	5	L. C. Jenner	6
C. P. Nickalls	5	A. Rawlinson	8
E. D. Miller	7	F. A. Gill	6
C. D. Miller	5	H. Scott Robson	5
	22		25

Ranelagh, June 22.

Final score: Rugby, 6; Ranelagh, 5.

Handicap makes no difference.

This is one of the cases where the question of ponies comes in handicapping Rugby. Something should be added to the aggregate for (1) ponies; (2) combination. To this it may be objected that this is to penalise combination. Yet in endeavouring to produce a handicap I think the opportunities of family teams for continual practice would have to be considered.

The advantages of the above system are obvious. It not only affords a perfectly fair way of classifying players, but also, as I have pointed out, gives us an excellent means of classifying tournaments, which naturally fall into four classes.

Thus:

Open tournaments not affected by the handicap at all.

Tournaments played under handicap divided into

    (a) Teams whose aggregate does not exceed 16.

    (b) Teams of all players below handicap No. 5.

Tournaments where the aggregate number is used as a means of classification, but which are otherwise played level, thus:

'This tournament open to teams whose aggregate handicap does not exceed' – (whatever may be the division decided on).

Tournaments in which no team shall play in which there is more than two players whose number exceeds six (or seven).

Novice cups and junior championships, all whose number does not exceed four or five.

Two questions have been put before me – one whether, when the entries are complete, the handicappers should not survey the teams in relation to each other; and, taking into consideration, for example, the amount of practice together any one team might have had, add to the aggregate points accordingly.

Example 10

England	*v.*	Wales
Smith		A. Evans
Jones		C. Williams
Robinson		B. Evans
Thomson		R. Evans
18		20

Wales, having three brothers and a total handicap of 20, might be raised to 22 on the ground of the opportunities for practice together, or because they had an obvious superiority in ponies. Or, again, England, retaining its number for the tournament, might be reduced by 2 to 16 in that particular match.

Indeed, the variety which a good handicap is capable of imparting to the game is very great, and it is just in sameness and monotony that the danger of polo losing interest lies.

For example, we see eight players at a match. They have no particular reason for being arranged, as they are, Mosquitoes v. Wasps. The Wasp will be a Mosquito tomorrow, and vice versa. They do not care much which side wins. Every one there knows the thing is a sham. They have not their best ponies, or, if they have, they are not really riding out – they are saving up for some open cup. When, for example, Roehampton won the Open Cup at Ranelagh, the four players in that team were in earnest to do their best – they had a natural patriotism for their club, and wished to win, and they played their best, and we all looked on and shouted, but we do not either shout or look on when the Redhairs *v.* Green-eyes are playing their little farce.

Another point which has been suggested to me is that the handicaps ought in some way to be modified by taking into account the ponies. The first thing to do is to ascertain what is the exact value of ponies to the game. It is commonly said that Rugby beat certain teams during the past two years by their ponies. We have seen that the victory of the English over the American teams in the international matches of 1902 was due in some measure to the superiority of the English ponies. This may be true, but the value of ponies is not perhaps quite so great as is thought, and it tends to decrease as the average of ponies goes up. But I think perhaps some distinction should be drawn between the resources of the dealer's stable and that of the private owner. All that can be done is to limit the number of ponies as is done by the Army Polo Committee, and to oblige the ponies to be entered as well as the players. That is, that the captain of a team should be bound to designate the ponies his team should play. But I think that it is quite easy to overrate the effect of ponies on the result of a match. Nor does superiority in ponies make up, as we saw last season, for the loss of one first-class player.

Rugby are the best mounted team, but all the speed and training of their ponies could not avert defeat when Mr George Miller was prevented by accident from taking his place in the team. My own feeling is, that beyond limiting the number of ponies to be used in a tournament by each team, and obliging the team to choose and specify beforehand by their registered numbers the selected ponies, we cannot go at present.

But it would not be difficult to devise a handicap for ponies thus:

Supposing ponies were divided into two classes, A and B, A to include all ponies that had played in a certain number, to be hereafter determined, of first-class tournaments, and B all the rest. Then the number of ponies to be played in a given tournament might be limited. This is the plan in outline that has been suggested by Major-General Douglas Haig, the Inspector-General of Cavalry in India, as a way of cheapening ponies in that country, but it is also a very effective handicap.

But I am more concerned at present with the objections that may be made to the handicap numbers for players, which is the main subject of this chapter. In the first place, it will be urged that the American system, of which this is a modification, has been tried at two well-managed Polo Clubs, Eden Park (in the Dewar Tournament) and Catterick Bridge, without any conspicuous success. But in both cases the team was taken as the unit, which is not, I am convinced, the right basis for a handicap, which should be based on a careful estimate of each individual player} If this estimate is fairly correct the total arrived at would be also approximately right.

The County Dublin Club had some success with their handicap in 1904, but the report is not very clear, and I think they too handicapped the teams and not the player. Moreover, casual and irresponsible attempts at handicapping are not very likely to be successful.

We want, if we want anything, an official handicap made by men having authority from the Hurlingham Club or County Polo Association.

But there is another objection which would naturally occur to everyone who knows polo. This type of handicap, it might be said, is based on individual play, and although this might be suitable for an open game like that of the Americans – a game which has no offside and no stick-crooking – it is not so for English polo. The American game favours the forwards, but English polo is based on combination and on defence. Team-play rather than individual brilliancy is its note. Therefore a handicap based on individual form is wrong in principle, and it would not work in practice, for the rate of scoring is so much higher in American polo than in English.

As to the first objection, I should reply that it is more specious than exact: all play at polo or any other game is based, not on any combination, but ultimately and in the last resort, on the skill of individuals. The splendid combination of Rugby could not win a champion cup in 1904 with Mr G. A. Miller out of the team. Where would the Old Cantabs be with Mr Buckmaster away? What happens when it is not Mr Freake or Mr Rawlinson's day, to the teams they play in? What did not Roehampton owe to Captain Herbert Wilson's rapidly improving form? These are but a few instances, but they are enough. Combination may be important at polo, but this, like every game, is based on individual skill, and that must be the basis of any handicap.

Then I find that the American players do not, as a matter of fact, make much larger scores than ours. Taking our provincial tournaments I note that the Rugby (1904) series averaged eight goals per match, and the average difference between the teams was three goals. At Leamington (1904) the averages were about the same. Cirencester (same year) averaged eight goals with an average difference of five between winners and losers. Taking seventy-two American games I find that the average difference was only four goals, so that there is in fact no such very great difference in the scoring in the two countries.

A handicap, then, is shown to be desirable and practicable, and I summarise the suggestions here:

(a)	That every player should have a handicap number assigned to him.

(b)	The highest number to be ten, the lowest two.

(c)	That in every handicap tournament the handicappers should be instructed to consider – (1) Whether a team is accustomed to play as a team; (2) How far the players are suited to each other, and are arranged in their proper places; (3)Whether one team is very much better mounted than the others. The handicap of the teams to be modified in accordance with those considerations, if the handicappers think it desirable to do so. Such modifications to apply to that tournament only.

(d)	The official handicap to be published on March 15th in each year, and to be in force for the following season.

(e)	Clubs offering prizes for handicap tournaments based on the official handicap, to publish in the public press the handicap of the teams entered, at least one week before the date of play.

(f)	All clubs or groups of clubs desiring to have a club handicap to forward the same for the approval of the Hurlingham Handicap Committee.

It has occurred to me that the County Polo Association and the Army Committee might have separate handicaps for tournaments played under their auspices.

I have written down these suggestions in a definite form, not as arrogating for them any authority, but because without definition and clearness no suggestions of the kind can be of any real value. They are only designed to incite others to consider and examine a subject which is of considerable importance to the future of polo.

14

The Rules of Polo in England

When polo came to England the game had no rules. The first regulations were the work of the Hurlingham Committee of 1872, and a comparison of those rules with the existing code will make clear to the reader how much the rules have developed since then. In the chapter on the early history of polo at Hurlingham I have shown how a fuller and in some respects a stricter code became necessary, and how penalties have grown in number and severity. The polo committee of the Hurlingham club has been the body that has made the rules, although the constitution of that committee has from time to time been altered, in order to give it a character more representative of the large and increasing number of players who are not members of the club. When nearly all polo players were members of Hurlingham, the general committee of that club appointed a sub-committee to regulate polo. This committee included the names of men who were among the leading players. Then, as clubs increased, the committee admitted the right of other clubs to send representatives to Hurlingham, provided always that the men who were chosen were members of Hurlingham. This was sufficient at the time. Most county clubs had one or more members of Hurlingham among them, and, even if the restriction had not existed, it would have been convenient to send those men as representatives to Hurlingham who were likely to be in town for at least some part of the polo season.

It was not until the year 1903 that the Committee was greatly enlarged, and a definite representation was determined on. Anxious no doubt to preserve the old association of Hurlingham with polo, it was determined that the members sent from other clubs should still be members of Hurlingham. In other respects the various bodies were free to send whom they pleased. It was left to the clubs and the County Polo Association to give what instructions they thought right to their delegates, and, in consequence, the last-named body has undoubtedly exercised a very considerable and salutary influence on recent revisions of the rules.

There has, since the South African War, been a revival of interest in various questions raised by the rules, and the latest revision of the code is an attempt to deal with some of the most important points which seemed to need alteration, or at least clearer wording. The general effect of the changes has been to bring the English rules more in accordance with those of the Indian Polo Association. The rules as revised are dealt with in this chapter, and each rule is commented on and explained, so far as is necessary, with reference to its past history and the state of the game at the present time. We must remember that it is by these rules that we have to regulate our play, and that it is important to understand them thoroughly.

HEIGHT

1. The height of ponies shall not exceed 14 hands 2 in., and no pony shall be played, either in practice games or matches, unless it has been registered in accordance with the Rules of Measurement. (Penalty 9.)

This is the first, and in some respects the most important rule of all. The original rule No. 1 laid down that the height of ponies must not exceed 14 hands. This regulation was never very strictly observed or enforced, for no attempt was made to organise the official measurement and registration of ponies. Every one played on any pony he could find. It is often said that many of the polo ponies played before the present rule was passed were 15 hands, and even more. I think there is some exaggeration about this statement, and that at no time was the average much over 14.2. I infer this from the small number of rejections which have taken place. The ponies do not look much smaller than they used to do, and we still hear remarks about the large size of ponies. Yet if we consider that every pony is measured under the Hurlingham conditions, and by men of the highest professional character and experience, we must feel that there is in reality very little room for error. Nor do I believe that any great amount of preparation for measurement in an objectionable sense exists. No doubt owners of ponies try to have them measured under the circumstances most favourable to passing under the standard. It is, moreover, the duty of the official measurer to pass a pony if he can, and it is in the interest of the game that he should do so. A pony, it is well known, does not at all times measure the same height. I remember one morning in India bringing a pony to be measured under West of India Turf Club rules. It was a cold morning and the pony had had a gallop. She was sent before the committee and measured 13 hands easily, though never before or since would she pass under the standard at less than 13.1½. But I have known instances of even greater variation. Yet, after all, the matter is not one of very great importance except to the owner of the pony, the value of which is considerably enhanced by the fact that he possesses a Hurlingham certificate. That which really makes a difference to the other players is the actual, not the measured size, and the weight of the pony, which is not much affected by small differences in a measurement so purely conventional as that of the height of a horse at the withers. We adhere to this way of measuring because no better can be suggested. Apparent variations in height are no reason for impugning the soundness of the system, and the Hurlingham certificate in a vast majority of cases represents within a fraction the true height of the pony. It does not in fact matter very much what the height fixed is, so long as we have a standard to which all must approximate as nearly as nature will allow. The 14.2 rule was passed in 1894, not without considerable resistance at the time. It was believed that any strictly enforced rule would reduce the already insufficient supply of ponies.

But as I have pointed out in a former work, the natural height of the horse is about 14.2, and there are many more animals of that height than there are of 14 or 15 hands.

The reason why the rule that ponies should be 14 hands was disregarded was that the supply at that height was found to be utterly inadequate. To have enforced the rule would have killed the game. The passing of the 14.2 rule gave a stimulus to the pony market, and made possible the operations of the Polo and Riding Pony Society.

The 14.2 pony was found to exist in hitherto unsuspected quantities, for about 14.2 was shown to be the height of most of the existing ponies. The rights of those who owned ponies above the new standard were safeguarded by creating a class of 'existing' polo ponies. A certificate was granted, without measurement, to all ponies played in certain matches before a specified date. This was obvious justice. Nevertheless murmurs arose that the rule was being evaded systematically in two ways. First, that ponies were prepared for measurement by methods which were cruel and unfair. The attention of the Hurlingham Committee was drawn by the P. and R.P.S. Council to the practices, or supposed practices in vogue. The members of the latter society being mostly breeders of ponies were much interested.

On inquiry the Hurlingham Committee found that, while the extent of such practices had been greatly exaggerated, there was some foundation for the charge. In any case the idea of such practices being in vogue depreciated the value

Mr Buckmaster and Mr Fowhall Keene, the champion polo players of two continents.

of the Hurlingham Committee's certificate, and several agricultural shows refused to accept it. The Polo and Riding Pony Society, however, gave useful support by accepting the Hurlingham certificate, and indeed making it compulsory for ponies entered in its stud book. At the same time I think that the picturesque stories of 'faking' were made too much of. Again the confidence felt in Sir H. Simpson, the late, and Mr Sheather, the present, official measurer, has contributed much to establish the Hurlingham certificate in its proper position.

The rule, however, was evaded in another way, which became easy as polo grew popular and the number of ponies employed increased. A pony which had been rejected or which obviously could not be measured, might be played, even at Hurlingham itself, and possibly in a tournament. Sold as a 'good polo pony' – for auctioneers take no responsibility as to whether polo ponies offered at their sales are registered or not – that had played at one or other of the first-class clubs, such a pony might easily, as some did and do, work its way into circulation as a polo pony. This has been met by adding a penalty of disqualification of the whole team in which such a pony plays, and thus practically throwing on the captain of the team the responsibility of seeing that the ponies are all registered. This, however, seems still to leave a loophole open for the introduction of ponies over height, since it is no one's business to find out whether the team has such a pony among possibly twenty or more brought for play.

The rule might be strengthened in two ways.

1st. That every captain when entering a team should deposit a list of ponies with their registered numbers. There need be no difficulty in changing one or more of the ponies if it is desired to do so, always provided the registered number of the substitute is given.

2nd. If auctioneers would insist on the insertion of the registered number of the pony in their catalogues when he has one. The absence of a number would inform buyers that the pony had not been measured, and put them on their guard. It may be added, however, that no prudent purchaser would buy a pony, unless he had first ascertained whether the pony's height was registered at Hurlingham.

UNSAFE PONY

2. No pony showing vice or not under proper control shall be allowed in the game. (Penalty 10.)

This is one of the most important rules, with regard to the safety of players. A vicious or uncontrollable pony is a constant source of danger. In my own experience many serious accidents have occurred as a consequence of a pony being under insufficient control. But this rule is now so carefully enforced, that it is very rare to see a pony at a well-managed club that is really dangerous to its rider or the other players.

Games are arranged at most county clubs known as 'cantering games' in which young ponies may be tested. But as a matter of fact it is not only wrong to bring a pony with a temper on to a polo ground, but useless, for such a pony will never play well. Sometimes, however, ponies develop vice quite suddenly, and I have known two cases of hitherto perfectly well-mannered ponies suddenly kicking in a game, and one of a hitherto blameless pony taking to biting. Such ponies would, however, be rightly allowed no second chance in any polo club nowadays.

GROUND

3. The goals to be not less than 250 yards apart, and each goal to be 8 yards wide. A full-sized ground should not exceed 300 yards in length by 200 yards in width, if unboarded; and 300 yards in length and 160 yards in width if boarded.

This rule establishes a minimum and maximum size for a match ground, and offers advice as to the size of a boarded ground. The dimensions of the polo ground were brought from India, but it was some years before there was a full-sized ground in England. The original polo ground at Hurlingham, though larger than its predecessor at Lillie Bridge, was still much smaller than most Indian grounds. It was then, as it is still (though it has been greatly enlarged and improved), of an irregular oval shape. Then came Ranelagh, and this was the first club to lay out a ground exactly of the size recommended here. I remember going over the match ground with the late Mr Moray Brown soon after he had become polo manager at Ranelagh, and after some trouble we succeeded in measuring out a ground that was 300 yards by 160 yards. In those days we should have liked another 40 yards of width. I believe this ground was at that time one of the largest in England.

However, the first full-sized ground that was made near London was at Eden Park. It was the experience gained on that ground that led polo players to think that a ground of less width than 200 yards was needed when the sides were boarded. The surface of an Indian polo ground is

A fall. The game is stopped by the umpire.

much harder and quicker than the soft turf of England; the bamboo-root ball is lighter than our willow-root one, and therefore is more likely to go out of bounds. But when men began to play on a full-sized ground in England, it was soon noticed that the ball went out but seldom – sometimes not once in ten minutes or longer. The pace at which good polo is now played makes ten minutes quite long enough for a period at polo, but, inasmuch as the bell is not rung to close the period until the ball goes out, it may often happen that ponies are kept going for several minutes over the prescribed time. The experience at Eden Park showed that the want of the intervals of rest afforded by the ball going out, were greatly missed by the players and ponies.

Opinion among players has wavered for some time as to whether 150 or 170 yards is the better width for a match ground. The former is probably the better, but 160 yards may perhaps hit the happy mean. Yet managers of county clubs and others, who may find a difficulty in securing a suitable extent of level ground, may take comfort in reflecting that while 300 x 160 is expedient, 250 yards in length and 24 feet between the goal-posts is all that is

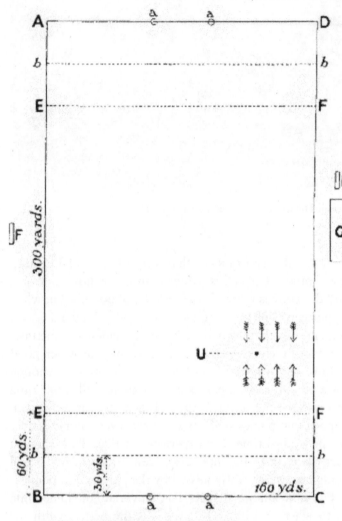

PLAN OF POLO GROUND.

A-B, D-C, Boards 300 yards long.
E-F, E-F, Line 60 yards from back line.
a-a,   a-a, Goal line 8 yards from post to post.
b-b,   b-b, Line 30 yards from back line.
G   Pavilion.
F, F,   Scoring boards.
U   Umpire bowling in new ball when former one has been damaged.

Plan of polo ground.

actually required. The question of breadth is left open. Yet there is no doubt that the dimensions recommended, which are the result of some years of experience, should be, as far as possible, adhered to in the laying out of new grounds.

This reduction of the size of the polo ground may be viewed with a certain amusement when we recollect that it was foretold, when the present Rule 1 was passed, that the increase in the height of ponies used would lead to great inconvenience, as it would certainly make necessary a general increase in the size of polo grounds. But it has turned out that a general decrease is the real effect of a fast game.

SIZE AND WEIGHT OF BALLS
4. The size of the balls shall not exceed 3¼ inches in diameter, and the weight of the ball shall not exceed 5½ ounces.

The balls used in England are made of willow- root, and are painted white. The present rule allows a slightly greater size and weight than the one before, but it probably only makes permissible the size and weight which have long been used.

UMPIRE/REFEREE
5. Each side shall nominate an umpire, unless it be mutually agreed to play with one instead of two; and his or their decisions shall be final. In important matches, in addition to the umpires a referee may be appointed, whose decision, in the event of the umpires disagreeing, shall be final.

WHISTLE/UMPIRE/REFEREE
6. The umpire shall carry a whistle, which he shall use as required. If the umpire blow his whistle the ball is dead, but if the other umpire disagrees, a referee shall be called in, who, after consulting both umpires and taking any necessary evidence, shall decide on the course to be pursued.

These two rules may be taken as one. Rule 5 is often broken. Matches are played without an umpire at all. It is very rare for the sides to nominate an umpire in England. In New Zealand it is not uncommon for a team, when on a visit to a tournament at another club, to take an umpire with them. The usual practice in England is for the polo manager of the club where the match is played to appoint the umpires. This seems to be the better plan, since it is undesirable that the sympathies of the umpires should be identified with any team. In India there are some very useful instructions to umpires, which are put out under the authority of the Indian Polo Association.

The most noteworthy addition to this rule is that when the umpire blows his whistle the ball is dead. The umpire therefore takes the whole responsibility of stopping the game, the moment he puts the whistle to his lips. No one but the other umpire may question the decision. The players must submit in silence.

If the other umpire disagrees, the referee who is to be appointed in all important matches – this word 'important' seems to need further definition – is to be appealed to. The referee may not often be called in, but, none the less, his is a necessary office. It is impossible perhaps to provide against all cases of injustice, but the following might bear hardly on a side: one umpire, A, gives a foul and blows his whistle, the other, B, disagrees. The referee, C, decides against A, but the ball is dead, and the mischief is done and cannot be repaired.

It is easy to imagine a case in which the side which was in possession of the ball might suffer considerable disadvantage from the mere fact of the game being stopped at that juncture. Nevertheless, the absolute prohibition of wrangling or argument is a great advantage. Umpires will do their work all the better, and give their decisions more freely if they are not to be called upon to give their reasons or hear outspoken condemnation of their decision by excited players. Moreover, it is obvious that there are some cases in which the second umpire could not disagree. For example, only one umpire is usually in a position to see an 'offside.' This, which is one of the points most often disputed, can henceforth scarcely be a subject for appeal. It is not perhaps likely that umpires will often feel obliged to exercise the severe penalty for disputing their decisions, which would almost certainly result in the loss of the match to the side that had a man disqualified.

TIME-KEEPER AND SCORER

7. An official time-keeper and scorer shall be employed in all games and matches.

The duties of the time-keeper and scorer are important, and should be entrusted to a person who can keep a clear head and will pay attention to what he is doing. In a close-fought game every moment is of importance, and the error of a fraction of a minute either way may cause a side to win or lose a match. The time-keeper must be provided with a stop-watch, and should use it carefully. As each ten minutes draws to a close he must be on the look-out to have the bell rung at the exact moment. Then he must estimate accurately the time that elapses between the ringing of the bell and the instant when the ball goes out of play. That time has to be subtracted from the next period, which, instead of ten, may thus be eight or seven minutes or less. This is particularly important in the penultimate period of a match, since the ball is dead and the game must cease on the first stroke of the last bell. In this case, thirty seconds added to or subtracted from the last period will make all the difference. Again, directly the umpire blows his whistle for a foul or an accident, the time should be taken. If the umpire decides to allow time, as he would do in case of an accident, or if a foul is given by one umpire, opposed by the other, and disallowed by the referee, the time must be calculated again. The danger is that the timekeeper, deeply interested in the match, may forget to start or stop his stop-watch at the right moment. The time-keeper generally combines the superintendence of the score. This, however, is made easy by the scoring-board and clock-face. The work of the scorer has been rendered more easy by the men who are placed at each goal to signal the passing of the ball between the goal-posts by waving a flag.

This is one of the many improvements in detail which we owe to the Ranelagh Club.

NUMBER OF PLAYERS

8. The number of players contending is limited to four a-side in all games and matches.

The reduction of the number of players to four a-side was, I believe, due to Mr John Watson, and I think he saw the advantage of this when playing in India.

On only one occasion was a championship played with five-a-side. The fifth man on either side was a goalkeeper pure and simple, and had little to do with the game until the enemy were pressing on his goal. Ten men overcrowded the ground, and it was only the skill of the early players and the absence of combination that enabled the games to be as good as they were. On the other hand games of three a- side are interesting and exciting, and not bad practice for forward players, but there is practically no defence, and there could of course be no offside.

This rule, simple though it looks, is really the foundation of modern polo, and has made possible the game of skill and combination we now know by that name.

The addition to the original rule of the words 'all games' as well as matches seems to point to a desire on the part of the committee to forbid or, at least, discourage three a-side games at any time. Indeed there is some reason in this, since such a game cannot be played in accordance with strict Hurlingham rules at all. At any rate we may take the day when the fifth man disappeared from our polo grounds as the birthday of the modern game, and the passing of this rule of four players a-side was the beginning of the faster pace, the closer combination, the more scientific tactics that make a first-class polo match so interesting alike to players and spectators.

HOW THE GAME COMMENCES

9. The game commences by both sides taking up their position in the middle of the ground, and the umpire throwing the ball into the centre of the ground between the opposing ranks of players.

There have been three ways of beginning a game of polo. The first and most ancient was to place the ball on a given spot in the centre of the ground. Then the two sides at a signal started full speed for the ball. I can remember this being the custom in India – at all events in Scinde, where I had my first experience of polo. After a time – and this was the usual plan almost up to the time I left India – the ball was placed on the ground in the centre. Two players rode up, crossed sticks in the air, and then there was a scramble for the ball.

The present way of starting the game is for the players to be ranged in the middle of the ground, and the umpire, mounted, bowls the ball between them. This should be done underhanded, the pony being moved forward a step as it is done, and it will be found that, with a little care, it is quite easy to avoid allowing any one to snatch the ball. At least the chance for each side is equal.

DURATION OF PLAY

10. The duration of play in a match shall be one hour, divided into six periods of ten minutes each, with an interval of three minutes after each period except the third (half-time), when the interval shall be five minutes.

EXCESS TIME

The five first periods of play shall terminate as soon as the ball goes out of play after the expiration of the prescribed time; any excess of time in any of these periods, due to the ball remaining in play, being deducted from the succeeding period.

LAST PERIOD
The last period shall terminate, although the ball is still in play, at the first stroke of the final bell, wherever the ball may be.

EXCEPTION
In case of a tie, the last period shall be prolonged till the ball goes out of play, and, if still a tie after an interval of five minutes, the ball shall be started from where it went out of play and the game continued in periods of ten minutes, with the usual intervals, until one side obtain a goal, which shall determine the match.

BELL
11. The bell shall be rung to signify to the players that the ten minutes has expired, and it shall be rung again when the ball next goes out of play, to indicate the time for changing ponies.

CHANGING PONIES
12. With the exception of the intervals allowed in Rule 10, play shall be continuous: any change of ponies, except according to the above provisions, shall be at the risk of the player. The period of actual play at polo, known in India as a 'chukker,' has altered considerably. In the members' games in India there was originally no particular time. The game was limited by the endurance of the ponies. In matches and tournaments a quarter of an hour was the usual time, and there was no particular time laid down for the intervals. In England the periods were actually at first, and nominally for some time, twenty minutes with periods of rest, generally of five minutes between each twenty. The close of the twenty minutes was a time of rest for the men,

but ponies were changed whenever it was convenient to the riders. It was all very friendly and pleasant. Someone would feel that his pony had had enough. This player would gallop off, and the others obligingly stopped. There was no rule about changing, or at least none that was enforced. After one man had gone, another one would think, 'Oh, well, I might as well change too,' and off he would go. Thus the delays and irregularities were endless, but there was no one to please but the players themselves. Polo had no public in those days. Directly public opinion, represented in those days by Mr Moray Brown, came to bear upon the game, it was seen that these irregular proceedings would not do. The ten minutes rule was the result. Nominally the periods were still twenty minutes, but the game was stopped at the end of each ten minutes in order that players might change their ponies. The increasing speed of polo and the advancing skill of the players made ten minutes as much as, and perhaps more than, any pony or man could do his best for. This rule met with a good deal of opposition at the time from some leading players. But it was strongly advocated by others and warmly supported in *Baily's Magazine*, wherein I was allowed to advocate this and some other reforms which have since come to pass. Next to the establishment of 14.2 as the standard height of a polo pony, this was in its effect on the game one of the greatest and most beneficial changes that have ever been made in the rules. The present rule acknowledges formally a change that had long ago been effected in reality. Polo periods are henceforward ten and not twenty minutes.

I look upon this change as only a step to the reduction, which I believe necessary and inevitable, of the periods to five minutes, and the total time occupied by the match to forty minutes instead of an hour. Already this has been done in India, and what the Indian Polo Association does today the Hurlingham Polo Committee is apt to do tomorrow.

These rules depend on Rule 7, in some measure, since the benefits of the rule and the equal bearing on the fortunes of both sides depends on the accuracy of the time-keeper.

The only safe time for a man to change a pony is when the bell rings, or if, during an accident, the umpires stop the game and allow time. There are, of course, other occasions when it may be worth the risk to change, such as finding a pony is not going well. Even the best of ponies do not always play-alike. Polo is a game at which we must take risks sometimes, and we may calculate which is the greater, to continue to ride an unsuitable pony or to gallop off to find another.

Of course, no consideration would induce a player to continue to ride a pony which is for any reason obviously unfit to continue to play.

There is an increasing tendency to ride but few ponies, often not more than three, or at most four being used, by each player in first-class matches and close games. A pony in condition can play three tens easily enough with intervals of rest of the same length. Most players, however, have a fourth pony to which they give a turn once in the game. But even in first-class polo it is a fortunate man who possesses more than two or three ponies on each of which he can play in his best form.

BALL HIT BEHIND BY ATTACKING SIDE

13. If the ball be hit behind the back line by one of the opposite side, it shall be hit off without delay from where it crossed the line, 1 after giving the opposing side reasonable time to get to the 30 yards line. None of the attacking side shall be within 30 yards of the back line when the ball is hit off. (Penalty 5.)

UNNECESSARY DELAY
N.B.: There must be no unnecessary delay. (Penalty 6.)

This rule has been separated from the following one which was originally a part of Rule 13. The two important points are that: (a) the ball shall be brought into play as soon as possible, (b) and the attacking side shall not be within 30 yards of the goal. The disposition of the sides is left entirely to the discretion of the respective captains, and it is open to any one of the defending side to hit out. This duty is, however, in practice always entrusted to No. 3 or No. 4, and in most cases it is No. 3 who hits out, No. 4 backs him up, and the forwards do their best to clear the way. It is a notable feature of modern polo that the defending side more often than not drive the ball away.

BALL HIT BEHIND BY DEFENDING SIDE
14. If the ball be hit behind the back line by one of the defending side, penalty 4 shall be exacted, provided the ball does not glance off another player or another pony. (Penalty 4.)

There was a time when no penalty at all was attached to this. It was not considered 'good form' to hit the ball behind your own back line in order to save the goal. But by degrees the custom of doing this crept in, and on one occasion at least the final tie of an important tournament was won by the judicious use of this expedient. Then it was decided to inflict a penalty. The side defending the goal was ranged behind the back line, whilst one of their number hit out from the centre of the goal-post, the attacking side being ranged outside a white line defining a semicircle 25 yards from the centre of the goal-posts. Hitting out to save the goal thus became an acknowledged part of polo tactics, since it was obviously better to hit out from any point than to have a scrimmage near the goal.

If the sides are fairly equal, and sometimes even when the side that hits out is the weaker of the two, there is a good chance of carrying the ball away from the hit out. The hit out from the centre of the goal-posts is no disadvantage, or at all events not so great a one as to deter players from saving their goal from danger by hitting behind.

The infliction of penalty No. 4 shows a clear intention on the part of the polo committee to discourage 'hitting behind to save your goal.' Penalty 4, 'a free "hit at" the ball from a spot opposite where the ball was hit behind, and 60 yards distant from the goal line produced, none of the side fouling to be within 20 yards of the ball. The side fouled being free to place themselves where they choose.'

This is a very severe penalty, and it defines the action penalised as a 'foul.' At the same time, and for this very reason, we must regard the rule as well thought out, since it places the goal in danger but does not make an addition to the score at all a certainty. As a matter of tactics it will still be worth considering how far it is safe to run the risk of incurring the penalty. We can all imagine occasions when it will be well worth while to do so.

BALL THROWN IN BY THE UMPIRE

15. When the ball is hit out, it must be thrown into the ground by the umpire from the exact spot where it went out, in a direction parallel to the two goal lines, and between the opposing ranks of players. There must be no delay whatsoever or any consideration for absent players. The ball should be bowled underhand in the same fashion as when starting the game. The last clause is intended to prevent the practice springing up of going off to change ponies when the ball goes out. A polo match ought to occupy an hour and a half, and it is desirable in the interests of the game that, except under special circumstances, this time should never be exceeded.

BALL OUT

16. The ball must go over and clear of the boundary line to be out.

GOALS

17. A goal is gained when a ball passes between the goal-posts, and over the goal line. If the ball is hit above the top of the goal-posts, but in the opinion of the umpire, between those posts produced, it shall be deemed a goal.

TO WIN GAME

18. The side that makes most goals wins the game.

ENDS CHANGED

19. Ends shall be changed after every goal, or if no goal have been obtained, after the third period.

Of Rules 16, 17, 18, 19, no explanations or remarks are needed.

RIDING OUT AN ANTAGONIST AND CROSSING

20. A player may ride out an antagonist, or interpose his pony before his antagonist, so as to prevent the latter reaching the ball, but he may not cross another player in possession of the ball except at such a distance that the said player shall not be compelled to check his pony to avoid a collision. (Penalty 1.)

DEFINITION OF CROSSING

If two players are riding from different directions to hit the ball, and a collision appears probable, then the player in possession of the ball (that is, who last hit the ball, or if neither have hit the ball, the player who is coming from the direction from which the ball was last hit) must be given way to. (Penalty 1.)

EXACT LINE OF THE BALL
1. Any player who follows the exact line of the ball from the direction, from which it has been last hit, is in possession of the ball rather than any player coming from any other direction.

LAST STRIKER
The last striker is in possession provided that no other player can, without causing the striker to check his pony to avoid a collision, get on the line of the ball in front of him. Under these circumstances the last striker may not ride into the adversary from behind, but must if necessary take the ball on the near side of his own pony.

LAST STRIKER
No player shall be deemed to be in possession of the ball by reason of his being the last striker if he shall have deviated from pursuing the exact course of the ball.

RIDING TO MEET THE BALL
2. Any player who rides to meet the ball on the exact line of its course is in possession rather than any other player riding at an angle from any direction.

RIDING AT AN ANGLE
3. Any player riding from the direction from which the ball has last been hit, at an angle to its course, has possession rather than any player riding at an angle in the opposite direction.

RIDING IN SAME DIRECTION
4. If two players are riding from the same direction, that player is in possession whose course is at the smallest angle to the line of the ball.

LEFT-HANDED PLAYERS
5. If two players are riding from opposite directions to hit

the ball, one of these being a left-handed player, the latter must give way.

N.B.: The line of the ball is the line of its course or that line produced at the moment any question arises.

This rule deals with important points relative to the safety of the player and the fairness of the play. Players we know are often not well acquainted with the rules, but everyone is bound to read over and to consider this rule and its various clauses in their bearing on his own conduct in the game. Rules must necessarily leave a great deal to the good feeling of players, and where that is not sufficient the umpire must step in. While granting that, in the excitement of the game, some players are reckless and unscrupulous; there is a tendency in the opposite direction which is to be deprecated. It is natural for men as they improve in skill and diminish in activity with age to advocate a less rough style of play. Moreover, the opinion of backs as to what constitutes roughness is sure to differ from that of young forward players. The Committee take the course of simply forbidding a few actions that are unfair or dangerous. Thus we see that players are left free to interpret the riding-out rule for themselves so long as they do not cross. It must, of course, be understood that all rules bearing on crossing and the possession of the ball only apply when the players are galloping. Fouls may be divided into two classes: (a) those that arise from improper riding of the pony, (b) those that arise from improper use of the stick. Those in (a) class can only take place at a gallop. There can be no crossing except it is necessary to check the pony to avoid a collision, and that implies a certain amount of speed in the first instance.

As to riding out, there are two opinions about the way this should be done. In India and in New Zealand the rule is that the ponies must be galloping alongside one another before riding out is permitted. In England there is nothing in the rules to prevent players bumping into one another at a considerable angle. In fact we have before now seen a player knocked clean over the boards. I think the English practice, though interesting to the spectators, should be forbidden because:

- It is dangerous to men and ponies. A pony was killed by a severe bump in 1904.
- It spoils the pony.
- It gives too great an advantage to big ponies and tends to exclude from polo a large number of useful animals.
- By favouring big ponies as against the smaller it makes polo more costly.

I know a player who preferred ponies of what we may call medium size, about 14.1, and of the light active sort. He tells me that now he buys ponies as big as possible, as he found the others were unable to stand the bumping.

The more necessary big ponies become the more difficult and expensive will it be to mount oneself at polo. The field of choice is by so much narrowed.

From riding off we come to crossing. The most frequent occasion of crossing is when one player is nearing the goal, and another on a faster pony is racing him and approaching at an angle. The ball must be diverted from its course or a goal is a certainty. The man approaching decides (quite wrongly) to take the risk, and either gallops across the front of the man in possession of the ball or interposes between him and the goal line. If in either case he causes the latter to check his pony, a cross is, or ought to be given against the man who intervenes. The cross is the most dangerous form of foul and the most frequent. The temptation to risk it is importunate at critical moments. Moreover, a cross is very often unconscious, the player's one thought is the goal, he forgets all about his relative position to the man behind him, so intent is he on the pursuit of the ball and the safety of his goal. But the penalties are severe, and in the revised code are more stringent than they were.

But you cannot cross a man unless he is in possession of the ball. Now if we study the wording of this rule we shall see that it is not so much the fact of having been the last man to hit the ball, as to follow in the exact line of the ball's course that gives the right of possession. Thus supposing the man who has hit the ball last, owing to a rebound from the boards or a bumping ground, leaves the exact line of the ball to shorten the distance he has to pass over before his next stroke, and another player follows the ball making the same angle as it does, the latter and not the former would be in possession and entitled to be given way to. Again, the man who is coming from the same direction as the ball is given preference over the one who is trying to meet it. But if both players are riding to strike the ball and the one meeting it is approaching the ball at a less angle than the one who follows, even though that player he the last striker, the man who is meeting the ball is entitled to be given way to. None of these provisions apply to left-handed players, who must always give way. In the Indian rules left-handed men are excluded altogether from the game.

We now come to a new provision which lays down that the last striker is in possession of the ball as long as he follows the direct course of the ball. It is, however, further provided that if another player can ride on the line of the ball without crossing or being convicted of doing so, the striker may not ride into him from behind. The effect of this is to deprive the striker, though he is keeping on the line of the ball, of some of the privileges of possession, since the wording, though very obscure, seems to imply that the man in front need not give way.

It will be evident on consideration that in practice this clause might deprive the striker of possession, for (1) if he cuts the ball hard the player in front will probably get it; (2) if he dribbles he may be caught from behind. Undoubtedly his best plan, if one of his own side is behind him, is to leave the ball for him and go right forward on to the player in front.

The latter is forbidden to ride into him; therefore the former need not give way. Henceforth the combination of a fast pony and an umpire not too keen will enable a player who may be unable to hit the ball to put a stop to a fast run. The last clause appears to have slipped in by accident. 'If necessary the player must take the ball on the near side of his own pony.' But under what circumstances is such a course necessary?

A little consideration will show that the player so situated will scarcely ever find it necessary to do this, except to avoid driving the ball into the pony in front, though he might find it convenient if he is good at the near-side forward stroke (which not one player in a hundred is). Most men would either leave the ball to their next man while they rode off the player in front, or would hit the ball away to one side or the other, and follow it as best they could.

This raises a nice point for the umpire. It is evident that at some period the man in possession must check his pony.

When does it amount to a cross? Again if the man striking and following the line of the ball is so near to the man in front that there is obvious danger of his striking into the pony's heels, then he must practically have lost possession of the ball as soon as this happens.

It is evident, though not from the wording of the rule, that this case might occur either on the line of the ball or that line produced. It seems as if the interposing player might hinder the striker without having much chance of obtaining possession himself. This rule may be justly criticised on the ground that it works in favour of back players, especially of No. 4, and against the No. 1. The rules want modifying and not strengthening in this direction. The Hurlingham Committee, being all back players, seem to have forgotten the necessary balance of the game. The great decrease in efficient forwards of late years might act as a warning that in a game of combination like polo we cannot upset the due balance of the backs and forwards without injuring the game.

DANGEROUS RIDING

21. No player shall ride dangerously. (Penalty 1.)

DANGEROUS USE OF STICK.

22. No player shall use his stick dangerously. (Penalty 1.)

23. In case of a player being disabled by a foul, penalty 8 may be exacted by the side that has been fouled, and penalty 1 shall be exacted in any case. (Penalties 1 and 8.)

ROUGH PLAY

24. No player shall seize with the hand, strike or push with the head, hand, arm, or elbow, but a player may push with his arm, above the elbow, provided the elbow be kept close to his side. (Penalty 1 or 2 or 3.)

DANGEROUS ROUGH PLAY

N.B.: Penalty 1 shall only be exacted if the umpire considers the play dangerous.

CROOKING STICKS

25. No player shall crook an adversary's stick, unless he is on the same side of an adversary's pony as the ball, or in a direct line behind, and his stick is neither over nor under the body or across the legs of an adversary's pony. The stick may not be crooked unless an adversary is in the act of striking at the ball.

STRIKING ACROSS AN ADVERSARY'S PONY

When two players are riding abreast, no player shall strike at the ball over or under the body or across the legs of an adversary's pony. A player who deliberately rides his pony up to an adversary who is in possession of and striking at the ball, or who deliberately rides his pony over the ball to prevent an adversary striking at it, does so at his own risk. (Penalty 2 or 3.)

A great number of accidents at polo are the result of blows with a stick inflicted on a player or his pony accidentally or through carelessness. Nor is it possible to get rid of this danger altogether at polo. As long as men are armed with such a weapon as a polo stick, accidents will occur from time to time in an exciting game like polo. The dangers to be guarded against are two: (1) from blows, (2) from the stick becoming entangled in the ponies' legs and thus bringing them down.

From the time I first began to write about polo I have constantly pointed out the suitability of the Indian rule which forbids striking out with the stick across a pony's forelegs in order to reach the ball. This has now been adopted. The modification of the stick-crooking rule which forbids crooking sticks, except when the player is in the act of striking the ball, is also borrowed from the Indian code of rules.

This change, which will meet with general approval from players, was inevitable. There is no doubt that it will make polo pleasanter to play. Nothing is more exasperating than when galloping after the ball with no immediate prospect of hitting it, to have your stick crooked from behind and possibly wrenched out of your hand.

Stick-crooking is not permitted in America, but Mr Foxhall Keene and other American players thought that it was an improvement to the game.

However, the present rule is plain enough. For the future it will not be lawful to crook an adversary's stick unless the stick is actually raised to hit the ball.

This rule will tend to prevent waving sticks, and perhaps there will be fewer infringements of the rule which forbids crooking over the pony's back. There seems little reason for an uplifted stick to be carried in the dangerous fashion so often seen.

All the rules about rough play are limited by the word 'dangerous', i.e. everything is lawful in a hustle or scrimmage (whether all things are expedient is another matter) unless the action be expressly forbidden (*vide* Rule 24), or be considered by the umpire to be dangerous.

It may be said that umpires will have different ideas on this point, but that is inevitable, and practice and custom will soon spring up, and the best players when umpiring will set a standard which by degrees will be accepted as the interpretation of the rule.

OFFSIDE

26. No player who is offside shall hit the ball, or shall in any way prevent the opposite side from reaching or hitting the ball. (Penalty 2 or 3.)

DEFINITION OF OFFSIDE

A player is offside when at the time of the ball being hit he has no one of the opposite side nearer the adversaries' goal-line, or that line produced, or behind that line, and he is neither in possession of the ball nor behind one of his own side who is in possession of the ball. The goal line means the eight-yard line between the goal-posts. A player, if off-side, remains offside until the ball is hit, or hit at again.

There is no rule that has been more discussed than this. There is no offside in the game as played in Manipur or Gilgit today. The American game has it not, and so far we have not convinced American players of the necessity of the rule. In India, on the contrary, players, both native and English, hold strongly to offside. But our own Polo Committee has not been very strong on the subject, for they have dallied with the alteration or even the abolition of the rule. No one, I think, had any doubts about the expediency of the rule until Mr T. B. Drybrough, in his excellent analysis of the rules of polo, drew attention to the discrepancies in the decisions of umpires on this point.

But no one doubts that in practice the decisions of umpires on the question of offside are very haphazard.

Putting aside a few of our best umpires, such as Mr Rawlinson, Captain Gordon Renton, and Mr T. B. Drybrough, the others for the most part either seldom give offside at all, or nearly always assent to a claim for it. If the reader will study the accompanying diagram, and will apply it to his experience of watching races, or possibly of judging, he will know how impossible it is to see which of the two horses has his head in front of the other at any given moment, unless we are quite parallel with them. Now this is a position which the best of umpires can seldom occupy. In theory the umpires should be two in number riding perfectly trained ponies, and galloping parallel to the 'back' of each side. In practice there is often only one, and he must do the best he can. Moreover, an umpire's attention must be fixed partly on the important duty of keeping out of the way of the players. In doing this he cannot always be in the most favourable position for observing what is going on. In reading the rules and studying them at our leisure, it must be remembered that polo is a game of rapid happenings and quick changes. Probably the umpires never actually see half the fouls and offsides that occur. Moved by these and other considerations, and also because polo is apt to become sticky when the zeal of a side for combined play is in advance of their skill in hitting the ball, the Polo Committee had doubts about offside. The open galloping game of the Americans was attractive. Probably it is better fun for all except the first-class players. The existing rule was, and is capable of several inconsistent explanations. A few games were played without 'offside,' but these trials were not very conclusive, and, as a matter of fact, several people had made up their minds on the subject before the trial matches were played at all. It was said that the game without offside was hard upon the ponies. It was understood that Indian polo players were certainly against a change in this rule. It was then suggested:

1. That offside should be more clearly defined, e.g. that the umpire must see the boot of the offender or the whole of the pony.

2. Instructions should be issued to the umpire as to the granting of offsides when claimed.

3. That (a) the penalties should be modified as being too severe, except in those cases which arise when a player chances being offside for the sake of the advantage to be obtained. Though scarcely justifiable, yet in the heat of the game forward players will do such things.

However, the rule was left as it was, but it must I think be dealt with some day. Probably the best plan would be:

1. To define what the umpire must see to constitute offside.

2. To modify the definition in the case of an offside which is occasioned by the action of No. 3.

There might be some difference between, as in the Indian Rule No. 27, the penalty for 'offside' when the result of reckless play on the part of the forward and offside when brought about by the tactics of No. 4. This player can, by checking his pony, often put No. 1 offside without any real fault on the part of the latter. The offside rule is already a sufficient advantage to the back, and it is inadvisable to strengthen in any way the defence, which is already so strong that it makes the game 'sticky' at times. It is in the closer definition of offside, or the relaxation of the penalties in the sense that I have suggested, that we are to look for the necessary improvement in the game. But I look forward still more to the growth of soldiers' polo to infuse into the game the dash and forward play that it requires.

27.	A player must not carry the ball.

In the event of a ball lodging upon or against a player or pony, it must be dropped immediately on the ground.

That is, a ball cannot under any circumstances be carried through the goal. There is a case in existence of the ball lodging under a pony's tail and being carried through the posts. But I should suppose that whether there was time to drop the ball or not no umpire would allow the goal.

STRIKING PONY WITH HEAD OF POLO STICK

28.No player shall intentionally strike his pony with the head of his polo stick. (Penalty 2 or 3.)

It seems a pity that the striking of a pony with any part of the polo stick is not forbidden. It is seldom or never done by the best players, and has a bad appearance. Were the practice to become common it would tend to bring the game into discredit, and this is sufficient reason for forbidding a practice which is bad for the player and his pony and disapproved of by public opinion.

BROKEN STICKS

29. Should a player's stick be broken, he must borrow one from one of his own side, or ride to the place where sticks are kept and take one. In the event of a stick being dropped, he must either pick it up himself, borrow one from one of his own side, or ride to the place where sticks are kept and take one. On no account may a stick be brought on to the ground. (Penalty 2 or 3.)

There is no rule more constantly broken than this. There is none that ought to be enforced more strictly. To see attendants or friends running about the ground with sticks is unseemly and dangerous. It is moreover unfair, for it certainly upsets the aim of players.

The old rule, in which the words from 'borrow one' to 'take one' did not occur, seems to me better than as it now stands, but this permission given to borrow a stick is seldom made use of.

DISMOUNTED PLAYER

30. No dismounted player is allowed to hit the ball or interfere in the game. (Penalty 2 or 3.)

I have never seen this rule broken nor any desire shown to join in the game by dismounted players.

THROWING IN BALL

31. If the ball be damaged, the umpire shall at his discretion stop the game, and throw in a new ball at the place where it was broken, towards the nearest side of the ground, in a direction parallel to the two goal lines, and between the opposing ranks of players.

N.B.: It is desirable that the game shall be stopped and the ball changed when the damaged ball is in such a position that neither side is favoured thereby.

Umpires should pay careful attention to the enforcement of the note to this rule. If a player is making a run and the ball breaks, as it often does, it should be left to the player to decide whether he will go on with the broken ball or have a new one. Any cries of 'broken ball' from the opposite side should be disregarded.

This is one of those accidents the disadvantages of which are part of the nature of things, so long as we have to play with brittle wooden balls. Many compositions have been tried, but nothing has ever come near to the spring and lightness of the willow-root ball. All others that I have seen are dead in comparison. The ball in use has only one superior, the bamboo-root ball of India, which is probably the best polo ball in existence.

ABSENT PLAYER

32. If a player leaves the game in order to change a pony,

or to get a fresh stick, or for any other purpose, the penalty for offside cannot be exacted against the opposing side until the return of the player into the game.

This is a new rule and should work well as a discouragement to changing ponies at odd moments. It is obvious justice to the side with four against three. The wording, however, is not very clear. What is the game? Is a man 'in the game' when he is on the ground? E.g. a player leaves the ground, then No. 1 cannot be offside. Does he become so provided he is in an offside position the moment the absent player re-crosses the boundary, even though the actual play may be going on two hundred yards away from the spot where the returning player is? This actually happened in an important match in 1904. It needs to be provided for.

33. No person allowed within the arena – players, umpires, referee, and manager excepted.

This is not always as strictly observed as it might be. Everyone will recollect in an exciting match at the Inter-Regimental how the crowd of soldiers, past and present, flowed over the boards on to the ground and half across it, to fly nimbly as the rush of the game brought the players down the boards under the pavilion. One often wonders that no one was hurt, or that the players never complained; possibly they sympathised with the enthusiasm of the spectators. But, though one may look leniently on the excess of keenness, the danger of the practice and its unfairness to players are obvious.

ACCIDENTS

34. (a) If a player or a pony be injured by a fall or any other accident, the umpire shall stop the game, and allow time for the injured man or pony to be replaced.

(b) If a player or a pony falls through that player or that pony's fault, the umpire shall not stop the game, unless he is satisfied that the player or pony is hurt.

WHERE BALL THROWN IN
N.B.: On play being resumed, the ball shall be thrown in where it was when the game was stopped, and in the manner provided for in Rule 15.

The only point to be noted here is that the umpire should be careful to tell the timekeeper that time is taken off, and that the latter should be careful to see this is done accurately.

SPURS AND BLINKERS
35. No blinkers, or spurs with rowels are allowed; no pony blind of an eye is allowed to play.

This rule is an improvement on the old one which allowed spurs with the permission of the Polo Committee. Blinkers are dangerous, spurs with rowels are cruel on most men's heels, and a pony blind of an eye is a danger to other players.

FOUL AT END OF MATCH
36. In the case of a foul occurring at the end of a match, and there not being time to exact the penalty before the final bell rings, 'one minute extra shall be allowed' from the time the ball is hit, or hit at, in carrying out the penalty.

This is new to the English code, but has for some time existed in India.

SUBSTITUTES IN TOURNAMENTS
37. In tournaments, if a player having taken part in the tournament for any reason be unable to play, he may, with the consent of the committee of the club where the tournament is held, be replaced by any player who, by the rules of the tournament, is qualified, provided the said player has not already competed in another team.

It might perhaps have been well expressly to exclude handicap tournaments from the last clause of this rule.

Polo managers know the difficulties of bringing a handicap tournament to a satisfactory finish. It would be one of the advantages of the handicap system advocated at an earlier page of this book, that it would be only necessary to select a player with a handicap number similar to that of the absentee.

DISREGARD OF UMPIRE

38. The decision and injunctions of the umpire must not be disregarded or questioned. (Penalty 7.)

This rule has been dealt with above, but it is a most desirable addition, as anything that strengthens the hands of the umpires must be. This is more particularly the case when we consider the increased weight of responsibility thrown on the umpire by the new rules.

INCIDENTS NOT PROVIDED FOR

39. Should any incident or question, not provided for in these Rules, arise, such incident or question shall be decided by the umpire or umpires. If the umpires disagree, a referee shall be called in, whose decision shall be final.

This gives umpires an absolute discretion as to the meaning of any rule not sufficiently defined. If it tends to more efficiency on the part of the umpires chosen, it will be a considerable advantage to polo.

PENALTIES

1. A free 'hit at' the ball from a spot 60 yards from the goal line of the side fouling, opposite the centre of goal, or if preferred, from where the foul occurred; all the side fouling to be behind their back line until the ball is hit, or hit at, but not between the goal-posts; nor when the ball is brought into play may any of the side ride out from between the goal-posts. None of the side fouled to be nearer the goal line produced than the ball is at the moment it is hit, or hit at. (See Rules 20, 21, 22, 23, and 24.)

2. A free 'hit at' the ball from where it was when the foul took place, none of the side fouling to be within 20 yards of the ball. The side fouled being free to place themselves where they choose.

3. The side fouling take the ball back and hit it off from behind their own goal line between the posts, none of fouled side to be within 30 yards of the goal line produced, the side fouling being free to place themselves where they choose. (For Penalties 2 and 3, see Rules 24, 25, 26, 27, 28, 29, and 30.)

4. A free 'hit at' the ball, from a spot opposite where the ball was hit behind, and 60 yards distant from the 'goal line produced,' none of the side fouling to be within 20 yards of the ball. The side fouled being free to place themselves where they choose. (See Rule 14.)

5. At the umpire's discretion a second free hit in the case of Rule 13 and Penalty 3 being infringed, and in cases when Penalties 1, 2, and 4 are infringed, a second free 'hit at' the ball. (See Rule 13, and Penalties I, 2, 3, and 4.)

6. In the event of unnecessary delay in hitting out the ball, the umpire shall call on the offending side to hit out at once; if the umpire's request is not complied with he shall bowl in the ball underhand, at the spot where the ball crossed the back line at right angles to the goal line or' goal line produced,' as hard as possible. In this case the penalty for an offside shall not be claimed against the attacking side should no one of the defending side be between them and the goal line produced, or behind that line. (See Rule 13.)

7. The offender warned off the ground for remainder of match, no substitute allowed to take his place. (See Rule 38.)

8. Designation of any of the players on the side fouling who shall retire from the game. The game shall be continued with three players a-side, and if the side fouling refuse to continue the game, it shall thereby lose the match. (See Rule 23.)

9. Disqualification of team offending. (See Rule I.)

10. The pony ordered off the ground. (See Rule 2.)

The penalties above collected together have a somewhat formidable appearance. There are ten of them as against three in the old code. There are now three different degrees of the free hit as against one. Penalties 1 and 4 deal with the free hit at 60 yards from the goal line. This is a sufficient distance from the goal line to prevent the stroke being absolutely certain to make a goal, yet not so far distant as to make it impossible to send the ball through with sufficient frequency.

It is, however, much more difficult to strike the ball through the posts when it is stationary than when it is moving rapidly over the ground.

Comparatively few free hits result in goals from the central stroke, though they often so improve the position of the side fouled as to lead to an ultimate increase of their score. Penalty 1 is more severe than Penalty 4, inasmuch as the side fouling may not stand between the goal-posts. Thus they have no chance of stopping a clean shot between their posts. Nor is this all, for the ball is allowed to be placed opposite the centre of the goal.

This penalty is inflicted for crossing (Rule 20), dangerous riding (Rule 21), dangerous use of stick, (Rule 22), for disabling a player of the opposite side (Rule 23), illegitimate hustling, but only when dangerous (Rule 24).

These offences are thus placed among the chief crimes of polo, and are accordingly punished with the greatest severity. They are also intended to prevent polo degenerating into an unnecessarily dangerous game.

Penalty 4, which I take next, is milder than Penalty 1, for the ball is placed 60 yards distant from the goal line produced and opposite the place where the ball went out. This penalty applies to the case of a hit out to save the goal by a hard-pressed side, and is new to the game.

Penalties 2 and 3 are alternative, and consist, in the case of Penalty 2, of a free hit at the ball from the place where the ball was when the foul took place, the side fouled not to be within 20 yards of the ball; and in the case of Penalty 3 the fouling side has to take the ball back and hit off from between its own goal-posts, the fouled side being not within 30 yards of the goal line produced.

These penalties are inflicted for:

1. Illegal hustling when not dangerous. (Rule 24.)
2. For crooking sticks in an improper manner. (Rule 25.)
3. 'Offside.' (Rule 26, except the last clause, which is only minatory.)
4. Carrying the ball. (Rule 27.)
5. Striking pony with head of polo stick. (Rule 28.)
6. Breach of rule as to broken or dropped sticks. (Rule 29.)
7. Interfering with the game when dismounted. (Rule 30)

The choice of the penalty depends upon the position of the sides at the time of the foul, and according to this a free hit is taken or the fouling side take back the ball to their own goal line.

I have in another part of this chapter given some reasons for thinking that in the case of Rule 26 (offside) the penalty is too severe. Indeed, I am not clear that this penalty is not too often permitted, and that Penalty 2 would not meet the justice of the case in a majority of instances.

The remaining Penalties, 5 to 10, explain themselves, and are intended either to discourage delay, or to meet cases of foul play or disobedience to rules referred to in the former part of this chapter.

Taking the rules as a whole, they appear to have one leading error running through them all. Wherever it is possible the back players and the heavy men are favoured, and the forward players, especially No. 1, are discouraged. This has several disadvantages.

(1) It makes polo more expensive, and places light men at a disadvantage.

(2). It keeps many men out of the game, for the position of No. 1 under the present rules is discouraging and mortifying.

It is often practically impossible for a No. 1 to do what he is told to do and ride off the No. 4.

(3) The natural advantages to the heavy men which are inseparable from the conditions of English polo, where soft grounds, often much cut up, are in favour of the heavy man and the big pony.

(4) It makes the games slower and therefore less interesting to the spectators, a matter of no small moment to clubs, which look for revenue from their gate money.

(5) No man can play No. 1 long without spoiling his ponies. This is notorious, and I wonder this fact alone has never suggested the advisability of a change. The game as played in England failed, as we know, altogether to commend itself to the American visitors, and players from India find it difficult to keep their form. What we want is

(1) The abolition of bumping at an angle.

(2) The excision of the paragraph referring to the last striker and the substitution of a more clearly worded definition.

(3) The modification of the 'offside' rule in such a way as no longer to give such overwhelming advantages to the defence, and to make No. 1's task easier and pleasanter.